820.9968 CLA
Clayton, Ann, author
African legacies, Afric
interviews and essays

MW01520786

GUELPH PUBLIC LIBRARY

African Legacies, African Fictions

Interviews and Essays

Ann Clayton

820,
9968
CLA

Clayton, Ann
    African Legacies, African Fictions: Interviews and
    Essays / Ann Clayton

Criticism.

ISBN: (pbk) 978-1-928171-68-3
ISBN: (ebk) 978-1-928171-69-0

Copyright © Ann Clayton, 2018

Cover Image is "Still Life" © David Wilhelm, 2018

Vocamus Community Publications

130 Dublin Street North
Guelph, Ontario
N1H 1N4

3 3281 02012 578 4

Contents

1. African Legacies, African Fictions   1

2. Interview with Ellen Kuzwayo   20

3. Interview with Obi Maduakor   32

4. Olive Schreiner: Life into Fiction   47

5. "A World Elsewhere:" Bessie Head as Historian   61

6. Olive Schreiner and Katherine Mansfield: Transformations of the Outcast Figure by Two Colonial Writers   78

7. White Settlers in the Heart of Empire: Visionary Power in Lessing's *The Four-Gated City*   92

8. Family and State in Prison Narratives by South African Women   102

9. Radical Transformations: Emergent Women's Voices in South Africa   113

10. Women's Writing: What's New in South Africa   126

11. White Writing and Postcolonial Politics: Nadine Gordimer and J.M. Coetzee   131

12. Posting South African Letters from Canada   146

Selected Bibliography   158
Acknowledgments   174
Biographical Note   176

Introduction

The interviews and essays collected here were written during the South African transition to democracy, and often delivered at Commonwealth conferences abroad, to explain that transition as it was expressed in South African literature. They should thus be situated within the power shifts of the early 1990s, when the African National Congress took power in South Africa. Black South Africans emerged as more vocal spokespersons for their previously silenced majority. A new generation of black women writers took the stage, with Ellen Kuzwayo's *Call Me Woman* as a marker and symbol of that transition.

South Africa began a new relationship with Africa, with South Africa as an African-led country. My opening essay on Ben Okri and other prominent African novelists was my attempt to broaden my own critical horizons and engage with them as a feminist critic. So was my interview, conducted after moving to Canada, with Obi Maduakor, the Nigerian Visiting Professor whose course I attended at the University of Guelph. He speaks strongly of the need to educate the majority of his people, and of African literature as tied to political liberation.

My essays on Commonwealth women writers developed out of my Ph.D research and articles on the life and writings of early South African novelist and global feminist Olive Schreiner (1855– 1920). I wanted to assess her writing as a sympathetic South African biographer and critic and later found many similarities and resonances within the stories of New Zealander Katherine Mansfield. They both wrote movingly of colonial childhoods, and made the family a microcosm of the nation.

Bessie Head is a powerful short story writer, novelist, biographer and historian who migrated from South Africa to Botswana and made it her adopted homeland. She records problems of rural development, male power in Africa, and village wisdom in Serowe. She blends journalistic and literary skills, and makes Serowe a global and African state and metaphor.

Doris Lessing left Southern Africa for England, for life and a writing career in London. I attempted to chart her writer's progress as a liberal southern African woman, from the racial violence of Rhodesia to the political cross-currents of London, and from realism to inward journals to science fiction. She has been a hardworking professional novelist, and a truth-telling woman writer. I found her perspective on the life of an ex-colonial woman living in London, the heart of Empire, illuminating and sympathetic as an ex-South African living in Canada.

The next group of essays seeks to describe the process of political and social change within the literature of the new South Africa, often written by African township-dwellers, and to explore the dialectic between art and political commitment. I wanted to situate this new generation, especially women, within theoretical debates about postcolonialism and postmodernism, which both question traditional ideas of the self, and the writer as a free agent. The women writers of the eighties and nineties were agents of information and self-revelation, writing with more urgency, and writing testimony about the violence of actual political change.

In the last essays, I compared Nadine Gordimer and J. M. Coetzee, South Africa's pre-eminent novelists, in terms of genres – European critical realism and post-modernism, and in terms of South African problems of race, sexual relations, state control, and women's liberation.

The last essay situates Canadian power relations and literature as a point of comparison to South Africa in terms of settler-indigenous relations, decolonization, and multiculturalism. Multiculuralism has been a founding fact in the 1867 establishment of Anglo-French Canada; a multiracial democracy was created in South Africa only in 1994.

The Association of Commonwealth Languages and Literatures conferences I attended in the eighties and nineties were significant landmarks in creating a forum for South African literature to re-enter the Commonwealth, as the country did, soon after democratization. I wish to thank the ACLALS and EACLALS organizers and publishers of these conference proceedings in Spain, France, England, Italy, Germany, and Singapore, where I had the opportunity to hear so many fine Commonwealth writers and critics. They were valuable places of literary critical training and debate, widening national horizons, creating new ties, and fostering multicultural understanding, now the creed and political platform of the Canadian Liberal government.

Another important forum has been provided by South African and Commonwealth publishers. In South Africa I am indebted to Heinemann, McGraw-Hill and Ad Donker, as well as the editors of journals such as *Current Writing* and *English in Africa*. Kirsten Holst Petersen and Anna Rutherford have been consistently supportive editors of Commonwealth writing, collecting the documents of South Africa as it approached democracy in a volume titled *On Shifting Sands: New Art and Literature from South Africa*, in which my article on South African women's prison narratives is included. Lauretta Ngcobo's piece in the same volume offers one of the few summaries of the problems of black South African women at a crucial time of political change. She expresses her hopes that the South African women's movement will fulfill its role as an influence on social change as "national selfhood" was approaching. Thanks to Victor Ramraj of *Ariel* for inviting me to guest-edit a 1996 *Ariel* journal on "Writing the New South Africa and to all of the excellent contributors.

In Canada, Vincent Massey, a former governor-general (1952-1959), speaks very eloquently about the position of Canada within the Commonwealth, one of his speeches collected in *Confederation on the March* being delivered at the opening session of H.R.H. The Duke of Edinburgh's Second Commonwealth Study Conference at the University of Montreal, May 15, 1962. 300 people attended, from 34 Commonwealth countries and territories. Massey speaks of Commonwealth collaboration as having some bearing on questions of global war and peace, and mentions Canadian pride in being"" the oldest nation in the Commonwealth." He also speaks in another essay of Canada as the founding nation of the Commonwealth in the creation of the confederation in 1867, and of the creation of the multicultural Commonwealth in 1947, when India became independent.

Massey quotes Queen Elizabeth II at Quebec in October 1964 as saying: "The function of constitutional monarchy is to personify the democratic state."

In his speech "To Meet the Commonwealth" Massey provides an early constructive suggestion about the strengthening of the Commonwealth Programme, which I hope will continue to expand. He points out, too, the valuable role that Canadian Prime Ministers have played in fostering racial equality, a role still being carried out by the current Liberal government, along with gender equality. This weekend's *Toronto Star* (April 1, 2018, A11) shows the continuing support Canada gives to African women, in a piece by Sally Armstrong on the wonderfully encouraging work done by Journalists for Human Rights, a Canadian media development organization. A recent workshop in Juba, South Sudan, was designed for training women journalists and to help them deal with problems in a state of civil war. Sarah Andrew is a presenter on their TV's Women's Forum, and other women leaders in these workshops are Anna Nimiriano and Irene Ayaa.

The New York Times International Weekly (March 31–April 1, 2018, p.15) also runs a helpful article for African women and children, by exploring 'The World's Most Neglected Crisis," by Nicholas Kristof, the Central African Republic, which faces severe conflict and malnutrition. He argues convincingly that conflict is the driver of extreme poverty, and mentions two aid agencies which would benefit by more international funding: Catholic Relief Services, and Mercy Corps. It is good to know that Canada is renewing its commitment to peacekeeping in its mission to Mali, as well as leading on international foreign aid to women.

The interviews and essays collected in my volume are intended to be a contribution to a further understanding of the literature of South African liberation, the place of South Africa on the African continent, the economic development and peace of Africa, and the friendships among Commonwealth countries, especially South Africa and Canada.

Ann Clayton, Guelph, Ontario, Canada, 2018

African Legacies, African Fictions

After we had walked a while, and when the wind lifted the edges of her wrapper, I asked her to tell me a story about white people. She said nothing at first. And then she said:

"I will tell you a story another time." We were silent. It seemed she had changed her mind.

"When white people first came to our land,' she said, as if she were talking to the wind, we had already gone to the moon and all the great stars. In the olden days they used to come and learn from us. My father used to tell me that we taught them how to count. We taught them about the stars. We gave them some of our gods. We shared our knowledge with them. We welcomed them. But they forgot all this. They forgot many things. They forgot that we are all brothers and sisters and that black people are the ancestors of the human race. The second time they came they brought guns. They took our lands, burned our gods, and they carried away many of our people to become slaves across the sea. They are greedy. They want to own the whole world and conquer the sun. Some of them believe they have killed God. Some of them Worship machines. They are misusing the powers God gave all of us. They are not all bad. Learn from them, but love the world."

– (Ben Okri *The Famished Road* 282).

Africa is still marginalized within debates about the new world order or the rethinking of critical paradigms in postcolonial theory. This is because Africa is still seen as a client continent, dependent on the affluent West economically and culturally. When "development" thought takes new directions, as it does, for instance, in the collection of essays by Marianne Marchand and Jane Parpart, *Feminism,*

1

Postmodernism, Development, it has to contest this burden of "development" thought and its objectification and marginalization of Third World subjects.

In the following discussion I outline a few major topics within African Studies. The first is the relationship between International and African Studies, where I draw on Phillip Darby's recent book, *The Fiction of Imperialism*. The second is the legacy of the nation-state in Africa, which Basil Davidson calls the black man's burden, and which I will be comparing with Fanon's conclusions in his earlier seminal work, *The Wretched of the Earth* (1961). The third refers to a few of the shifting paradigms which have occurred in critiques of gender and nationalism, and analyses a few key works that have appeared in postcolonial theory and diaspora studies in Canada, in order to set up some terms for comparative international debate.

I. International Studies and African Studies

Phillip Darby, in his comprehensive 1998 study, *The Fiction of Imperialism*, addresses the ideational and instrumental value of literature in imperialism and decolonization. He suggests that the theory of international relations took over from imperial history, and that world systems theory and globalization discourse come from an empirical, positivist tradition which marginalized literature. Similarly, deconstruction and an arcane theoretical vocabulary may not be appropriate to a critical practice concerned with the destructive power of colonization, especially in places such as Asia and Africa, where the major effects of colonialism are endemic poverty and illiteracy for the masses. He seeks to reconnect the personal and the political, interrogate the dimensions of economic interest and power politics in literature, and, in his discussion of the African context, to link cultural expression more firmly to politics.

His critique can be supported by a brief look at a few turning points in the criticism of African fiction. Wilfred Cartey's *Whispers from a Continent* (1969) established a thematic typology for the African novel, charting a movement from the failure of assimilation to revolt to the awakening of national consciousness. Because of the date of his work, the later period of post-independence disillusionment in Africa and the complex theorizing of nationalism itself (by

Benedict Anderson, Etienne Balibar, Homi Bhabha, Basil Davidson, Eric Hobsbawm and Tom Nairn among others) could not be taken into account. Eustace Palmer's work on African fiction, published in 1972 and 1979, favours New Critical approaches in order to contest the universalizing tendency of conventional critical models.

Charles Larson's detailed scholarship in *The Emergence of African Fiction* (1971) sees certain key socio-economic shifts expressed in African literature, from rural to urban life, from communal to individual experience, and from an oral to a written tradition. He discusses the problems of the European literary reception and assessment of African fiction, an enduring topic, but is himself inclined to use a Eurocentric definition of the novel as a norm. Novels, in his view, are concerned with "man in social relations" in a contemporary realistic setting.[1] African novels are then characterized in terms of lack: there is a lack of character development and credible psychological motivation, and there are two main plots, the first being a loose narration of events and tales, the second being a situational plot where an entire group is affected by the main event, as in Ngugi's *Weep Not, Child*.[2] Larson goes on to defend African literature in terms of cultural distinctiveness, and argues that the African writer has created new unities, forms and patterns. He reads Achebe's foundational *Things Fall Apart* as a narrative about a man outgrowing an African epistemology, and a warrior code of manliness, in an African process of cultural syncretism.[3]

I would argue that the crisis around masculinity in *Things Fall Apart* expresses cultural crisis, and points to the difficult nexus of gender codes and African patriarchy at the advent of colonial dispossession. Colonialism intensified masculinist fears and self-assertions towards women and children and Okonkwo's wife-beatings and the killing of Ikemefuna, his foster-son, gives a politically charged meaning to traditional sacrifice, associating it with the pressures of the colonial encounter. In the same way Okonkwo's punishing exile, though prior to the colonial encounter in narrative sequence, marks the historical moment of cultural alienation for Africans, and anticipates a future of many exiles and displacements under colonialism. Rituals of propitiation and ceremonies of cleansing and purification, which are here associated with deviations from traditional belief, would be

3

reworked in the post-independence fiction of Nigerian Wole Soyinka and Ghanaian Ayi Kwei Armah, which critiques the corruptions of the post-independence African state and its leaders.

What I want to argue for, in reading African fiction, is a recognition of the strength and continuity of forms of colonialism in colonized cultures, but also the continuity of forms of African creativity and agency. Neither of these forms of continuity is served by a model which separates a traditional African from a Western culture, either by subordinating the former in a mode of savagery or permanent dependence, or exalting it in the essentialism of Negritude. These have been the two major attitudes to African literature, the latter responding to the liberal custodianship and Eurocentric patronage of the former.

Charles Larson, who embeds his detailed critical analysis of African fiction in social contexts, traces the relationships between a popular didactic literature in Nigeria, the pulp writing of the Onitsha market, and the works of prolific novelists such as Cyprian Ekwensi and Chukwuemeka Ike. Popular Nigerian literature is that of people new to an urban environment, and the mixture of true confessions and didactic advice expresses a response to urban conditions. The Kenyan novel, Larson suggests, begins later with Ngugi's *Weep Not, Child* (1964), whereas the African novel was pioneered earlier in West Africa, and began there, with Tutuola's *Palm-Wine Drinkard* (1952). This opinion seems to disregard the earlier history of fiction in South Africa, with Sol T. Plaatje's *Mhudi* being written in 1917, though only published in 1930 and with the very limited circulation of a small missionary press. South Africa, partly for historical and political reasons, has usually been treated as a discrete political and cultural unit in Africa. Larson continues this tradition, mentioning, as South African differences from tropical Africa, the longer-established ties with Europe and education in English, less influence from oral and communal African traditions, the overriding theme of the inhumanity of racial oppression, the greater presence of women and love relationships, and the novel as an extension of the traditional English novel.[4]

There is some truth in these differences, but the parallels between Ngugi wa Thiong'o's Kenyan literature of Mau Mau liberation struggles and the South African resistance fiction of the seventies and eighties are quite strong. Both Kenya and South Africa have been multi-racial settler societies under predominantly British rule, but even Nuruddin Farah's depiction of underground politics and conspiracies in Somalia, and the parallels he invokes between patriarchy and state autocracy, bear comparison with East and South African liberation politics and fiction. The similarities are rooted in the similar conditions of colonial oppression of an African majority, the scattered and then more unified illegal responses to oppression, and the autocratic and militaristic reaction to any organized political opposition.

Kenneth Harrow's *Thresholds of Change in African Literature: The Emergence of Tradition* (1994), offers a good example of both positivist and deconstructive critical approaches to literature. A scientific model of paradigmatic change by sociologist Thomas Kuhn is utilized, and Harrow invokes a critical tradition from Barthes to Derrida. A critical reliance on the infinite play of signifiers tends to loosen critical discussion from economics, politics and the history of colonialism in Africa. Africans are located as ambiguous adventurers within an ambivalent subjectivity. The specific continuities and effects of colonialism in Africa, which are the overriding themes of African fiction, tend to get lost.

Phillip Darby's discussion of Africa asks a key question: "what course is to be negotiated between the pressures for international standardization and the claims of cultural distinctiveness?"[5] Africa has been referred to as the sign of the exception in comparative studies (as South Africa has in postcolonial theory) and has continued to operate as "the repository of certain repressions and projections."[6] Even in contemporary fictions such as Margaret Laurence and Isabel Huggan's, literary evocations demarcate Africa as a place where Canadian sensitivities are made uncomfortable: by the circumcised and exploited girl children of Somalia, and by the master-servant relations of East Africa. Africa marks the boundary of Canadian 'civilization' and tolerance.

These Canadian texts, Laurence's *The Tomorrow-Tamer and other Stories, This Side Jordan, The Prophet's Camel Bell* and Huggan's *You Never Know*, are literary evocations of cross-cultural tensions between European development discourse and African underdevelopment. They also point to different patterns of colonization and internal colonialism in Africa and Canada, and to issues in comparative ethics, such as female circumcision and the sexual exploitation of children, which are difficult to resolve and which continue in the life of immigrant minority communities in Canada. The further Western ethnography has gone in dismantling any absolute perspectives on difference and otherness, the more difficult it has become to make any moral judgements and legal decisions on such practices in multicultural societies.

Though some feminist critics have addressed the silences and gender biases of African fiction (Boehmer) there are insufficient critical linkages between female circumcision, polygamy, wife-beating, the eliding or silencing of female presences in benchmark novels such as *Things Fall Apart*, the derogatory or constantly eroticizing discussions of women in the work of Soyinka, Ekwensi, and much popular African fiction, or the symbolic usage of female reproduction, fertility, motherhood and even polygamy to render the processes of political liberation or cultural reconciliation for male African novelists. Only Anne McClintock has fully argued the case that national constructions have rested on powerful constructions of gender, and that this imbrication has not been recognized.[7] However, not much has been made of these physical and narrative excisions of females in Africa and their parallels with other silencings of women and their sexuality, and their political voices, in Western literary canons and in some critical paradigms, such as Harold Bloom's patrilineal models of literary influence and tradition (1973). In Bloom's critical model, literary fathers and sons, much like Okonkwo and his sons in the village of Umuofia, wrestle eternally for dominance. These critical and creative parallels underline forms of continuity between Western and African patriarchy.

Darby's questions address themselves to the novelist's use of the past, ideas about community and pan-Africanism, everyday life, approaches to the modern nation-state, and Africa's responses to modernity. He cites Simon Gikandi's argument that texts like Chinua Achebe's are not contained by a realistic mode, but reorganize African cultures and "create a mythical space within which a new social order can be evaluated."[8] He asks: "has the modern nation state been domesticated within African literature?"[9] To answer this question one can turn to the comprehensive work on the African nation-state done by Basil Davidson in *The Black Man's Burden*, and Fanon's analysis of the dialectic of liberation struggles in Africa. These works provide a generic framework for an understanding of colonialism in Africa, and the forms of liberation politics.

II. The Legacy of the Nation State and the Dialectic of African Liberation

In Davidson's work, Africa's social crisis is directly related to the crisis of institutions within which Africans have been forced to survive after decolonization. States were built on alien European models and had little legitimacy for the African majority, who turned to "clientelism",[10] a dependency on networks (tribal, familial, and personal) which sowed chaos after independence. This system reflects the pathology of the postcolonial or neo-colonial state. The search for answers began around 1850 with the Atlantic slave trade, when "recaptive" slaves became the first literate intellectuals of precolonial Africa. Pressure from this fifth column brought an articulation of a future restored African sovereignty into British imperial doctrine. Who would be Britain's legatees: traditional custodians of power, chiefs and kings, or the modernizers? This question is still at the heart of enquiry in many post-independence African novels. The modernizers saw African peoples as being transformed into nation-states on a European model. A Gold Coast clergyman, Attoh Ahuma, used the familiar colonial phrases "savage backwoods" and "darkest Africa" as the conditions to be escaped in order to move Africa "into the open where nations are made."[11]

In the 1870s, as we know, the British and French turned sharply to military enclosure, and by the end of the century Eurocentrism and the ideology of racial superiority were paramount. Unlike the French, the British did not hold out empty promises of assimilation or lecture on the rights of man. The Belgians followed the French model. The Italians, Spanish, and Portuguese covered colonialism in a miasma of Christian beatitude. Acknowledged chiefs became the agents of foreign domination (there is a resonant portrait of a semi-modernized chief in Nadine Gordimer's *July's People*). Intellectuals were seen as subversives and chose or were forced into exile.

Davidson uses the precolonial model of the Ashanti polity, with mythic origins and symbols, and a typical self-adjusting political system and charters of self-identity, to illustrate a failure to adapt to modernization and colonial enclosure. Trading contact with Europe was culturally narrow and was narrowed more by the slave trade. There was no time for adjustment. The British policy of enclosure and dispossession froze indigenous institutions and robbed colonized peoples of the scope and freedom for self-development. People were degraded to migrant workers and semi-slave labourers.

The dichotomy of tribalism versus democracy is thus a Western imposition. The history of so-called precolonial tribalism was really a history of nationalism. This reading provides an oppositional platform to the lingering colonial influence, quite marked in Western media, which treats all African problems as if they are an expression of regression to tribalism. The African Iron Age in about 500 BC, when metal technology began in central and western Sudan and the Upper Nile valley (and partly superseded the farming era from 6000 BC) fathered the diversity of African culture. The third phase, in mid-nineteenth century, brought European dispossession. In the remote past great spiritual dramas were played out in ritual dance and song which celebrated human survival against the mystery of death. New problems and cultural conditions needed new modes of psychological reassurance. This context enables one to read the African novel, arising as a partly European literary mode just prior to the independence of African countries, as a genre which would carry the contradictory cultural experience of colonialism and decolonization, harnessing the oral tradition among others to retell Africa's past, rehearse the present, and carry forms of community and solidarity into the future.

Amos Tutuola's *The Palm Wine Drinkard* (1953) can be read in this way rather than as an expression of illiteracy or total naiveté. The loss by the drinkard of his tapster expresses cultural loss, the loss of pleasure among companions, the breakdown of access to material and spiritual resources, and the beginning of the exploitation for foreign interests of indigenous resources. As palm oil is the major West African export and source of commercial power, the drinkard's lack of access to customary resources can be read in this materialist way, as symptomatic of a breakdown in traditional patterns of local resource and community. The narrator's visionary journey to the

Deads' Town is both an expression of Yoruba myth and a summary of the everyday difficulties, power struggles and search for the means of survival in Africa, a quest which underwrites much contemporary African fiction. As Michael Thelwell points out in his introduction, Tutuola translates conventional folktales into the idiomatic English of the Nigerian masses, and thus prepares the way for Achebe's similar achievement in carving out a new African amalgam of language, dialect, myth and symbol to render cultural upheaval and transition. Metamorphosis plays a crucial, repetitive role in the narrative, evoking spiritual power, fear of the unknown and victory over strange assailants.

The Palm Wine Drinkard generates a narrative energy leading towards a redemptive sacrifice and an end to famine; this pattern is both mythic and political in Africa. The slave who takes the sacrifice to heaven does not make it back to his house because the heavy rain begins, "but when for three months the rain had been falling regularly, there was no famine again."[12]

African fiction finds the cultural means within its own spiritual and cultural traditions to transform suffering and deprivation into sacrificial radiance and power.

Ben Okri, the heir to Tutuola's vision, writes forty years later that Africa holds "the secrets of transforming anguish into power."[13] In Okri's masterpiece, *The Famished Road* (1991), the spirit-child, the "abiku" child abhorred by traditional Igbo society, becomes a visionary and charming narrator, living between two worlds, the visionary and the mundane, and able to perceive a historical past and potential future for Africa. The episodic narrative is structured on an insistent repetition of conflict, violence, wretchedness in multiple forms, and repeated visionary moments arising out of daily strife, with moments of cumulative wisdom and grace, as in Azaro (Lazarus's) mother's parable on colonialism,[14] and in the novel's final celebrations of struggle, the world of recurrence that the spirit-child symbolizes, "an unwilling adventurer into chaos and sunlight, into the dreams of the living and the dead."[15]

Okri, perhaps because he lives in London and writes from exile, does not seem to be a part of the despair and alienation expressed by most post-independence writers living in Africa, such as Ghanaian Armah's *The Beautyful Ones are not Yet Born*, where excrement and filth image the corruptions and collusions of post-independent Ghana. In Soyinka's *The Interpreters* the drowning of parents in the opening scenes invokes a lost world of care and traditional humanity; the present is taken up with drunken wrangling in a pub, quarrels, exploitative sexuality, and political despair. Davidson reads the causes of this post-independence condition in the consequences of nation-state construction, a conflict between the good of the nation and the people, the milking of peasant labour for foreign profits, a petty-bourgeois nationalism, elitist rivalries, the lack of middle strata, the whole colonial legacy become a coil of problems. The shift from the countryside to an urban periphery and shantytowns, and rapid population growth added to social problems. This crisis of social disintegration was framed by the Cold War, the contradictions of Soviet policy in Africa (defending an Angolan republic against the military aggression of South Africa but buttressing a military dictatorship in Ethiopia), and the capitalist neo-colonial stance of the United States. The party political model derived from European class structure did not fit African realities. The city triumphed over the village; state patronage, bureaucracies and armies grew, and so did the gap between a small wealthy minority and an impoverished rural mass. The triumph of South African Lauretta Ngcobo's 1991 novel, *And They Didn't Die*, lies in revealing the passage of rural people into politicized awareness over decades of opposition in South Africa. Nigerian Ben Okri's *Famished Road* uses the generic structure of the village compound as the basis of his narrative setting for one family as microcosm of African life, in order to highlight a cultural pattern of everyday struggles for food and survival.

Davidson draws a parallel between the African pattern and the disintegration of Soviet hegemony in Eastern Europe, not into bourgeois democracy but into military dictatorships. The national question of state power overrode the social questions of moral and material improvement, the results being stagnation and political repression. The lack of true citizenship in Africa has been reflected in post-independence realism as well as in Okri's use of the surreal and magical. There are only two political parties in *The Famished Road*: the Party of the Rich and that of the Poor, and Azaro's central milieu is

Madame Koto's bar, which eventually becomes a brothel and makes her very rich. Davidson suggests that a truly post-imperialist future would have to be a federalizing future and quotes German Erhard Eppler, who found it encouraging "that national identity is no longer tied to nation states, or even aims at creating nation-states, but is often rooted in older kinds of community."[16]

Frantz Fanon's 1961 study of the dialectic of colonial struggles in Africa, *The Wretched of the Earth,* agrees with Davidson's view that the political party system is an import to Africa, but draws economic and ethical conclusions from the history of colonialism. The former colonizers should pay their debt and rehabilitate the formerly colonized peoples. Fanon argues that there was a movement from tribalism in the colonial phase to regionalism in the national phase. The dream of freedom is found in the hearts of the peasantry. This is borne out by African fiction, especially Ngugi wa Thiong'o in Kenya, Peter Abrahams, Alex la Guma, Mongane Serote, Sipho Sepamla, Miriam Tlali and Lauretta Ngcobo of South Africa; Chinua Achebe, Amos Tutuola, Wole Soyinka and Ben Okri of Nigeria, Nuruddin Farah of Somalia, and others. As Darby points out, contemporary African writers and thinkers such as Farah and Soyinka, as well as Achebe, have made substantial contributions to rethinking the African state, once taken to be the vehicle for national liberation .[17]

Fanon describes one function of culture as "to create the new rhythm of the nation" by representing "the dialectic of armed struggle for liberation."[18] The urban spearhead of revolution is found in the people of the shantytowns, which is why South African Peter Abrahams's 1946 novel, *Mine Boy,* is so crucial to the literature of anti-colonialism, because it depicts not only the process of urbanization and the barring of significant citizenship to Africans in the cities, but also the moment of multiracial opposition crystallizing directly out of labour and economic relations. With the rehabilitation of the colonized, which is partly a cultural process, the people "march proudly in the great procession of the awakened nation."[19]

Fanon's analysis of the post-independence situation in Africa is that nation is passed over for race, and tribe is preferred to state. There is a failure by the national middle class, which in any case lacks much real economic power, to understand popular action. He concludes that the national middle class should put its intellectual and technical expertise at the service of the people. The explanation of postcolonial fiction in Africa lies in the failure of the African bourgeoisie. Old territorial realities and racial hostilities surface at independence, because colonialism, being bent on economic profit, developed only very localized resources. Thus any national unity created in liberation struggles gives way to regional interests and conflicts. Colonial power continues after independence through a national bourgeoisie, their control of the army, and national dependence on foreign capitalist interests.

Fanon states: "The efforts of the native to rehabilitate himself and to escape from the claws of colonialism are logically inscribed from the same point of view as that of colonialism."[20] When a native intellectual affirms culture he affirms a broad African culture; he has to demonstrate that a Negro culture exists, because all thought has been racialized by colonialism. The concept of negritude was the emotional antithesis of the racial insult of colonialism. "The unconditional affirmation of African culture has succeeded the unconditional affirmation of European culture."[21] This is where philosophies of blackness and Africa overflow continental limits and link up with Afro-American voices, but often in an essentialized gesture. It is, however, the national struggle for liberation that sets culture moving and creates self-consciousness.

My own view of the debate around the nation-state, after researching the fiction of South Africa and national narrativization, is that the 'nation-state' is a hyphenated fiction. The power of the state is always co-opted by sectional interests or a dominant group; in cultural expression the state has been romantically conflated with the nation in ways which mystify economic dominance and class interests. This can be seen in the romanticization of cross-racial friendship in Alan Paton's *Cry, the Beloved Country* (1948), written just as the apartheid state was being set up. The liberalism of Anglo-South African fiction masked a conservative collusion with the policies of racial segregation and the tribally based homelands system. The transactions of patriarchy also masked the gender dominance in both conventional colonial marriage and in the capitalist exploitation of African labour, a pattern which is much clearer in Paton's second novel, *Too Late the*

Phalarope (1953). In the famous S.G. Millin novel, *God's Step-Children* (1926), family tropes mystify the historical racial mixing which became the legalistic proscription of the apartheid state. The foster-child trope also sentimentalizes and conceals the biological basis of Millin's racism in her imagery of decadent "blood-mixtures". The "mystery" of European regression and loss of control in Africa, rendered in sublime prose by Conrad's *Heart of Darkness* at the turn of the century, is given a biological underpinning in Millin's work in South Africa in the decade leading up to Nazi Germany and its politics of eugenics.

If one were to translate this kind of analysis of a cultural unconscious into Canadian terms, taking Sinclair Ross's *As For Me and My House* (1941) as a founding text, the transactions of a married publically Christian couple with a single woman, Judith West, symbolize the transactions of a Puritan settler ethic with a world of desire and fertility, a world that the closed horizons of Horizon have excluded, choosing narrow social propriety and religion over art and sensuality. The novel ends with the adulterous woman punished by death, the married couple rejuvenated and with the child born of the love affair adopted by the previously emotionally thwarted wife. *As For Me and My House* renders the textual and sexual unconscious of a narrow pioneering ethic in settler Canada, which partly explains its continuing power. A comparison with Paton's *Too Late the Phalarope* indicates very clearly how the third figure, that of the African woman in Paton's text, is represented in terms of class and economics in Ross's novel (Judith comes from shiftless folk and is disapproved of by the middle-class moralists of the town). The terms of Canadian criticism, traditionally set up around relationships with the United States and imperial Britain, and in quest of paradigms organized around cultural nationalism, landscape and environment, have not favoured this kind of critique, which does highlight the representative relationship of women to economic interests, class and national structures, whether the labour force forms a racial majority or not.

III. Gender and Nationalism, Canadian Comparisons

In Andrew Parker's *Nationalisms and Sexualities* (1992) the authors point out that traditionally nation and sexuality have been treated as autonomous and discrete. National was conflated with public identity, sexual with private behaviour. The work of Foucault, Lacan, and Homi Bhabha in postcolonial theory, has alerted us to the ways in which the proliferations of modern nationalisms in Europe influenced the construction of middle-class norms of the body and sexual behaviour, and demonstrated how these codes of bourgeois morality could facilitate in turn the rise of fascist nation-states in the twentieth century. This insight could be further applied to the literatures of colonialism and decolonization. I have recently suggested in an analysis of Alice Munro's new collection, *The Love of a Good Woman*, that her attention to the profane, unclean, transgressive and accidental aspects of sexuality marks democratizing tendencies in her work, just as her breaking of mimetic codes marks the space of gender-coded conflicts in women, between their social construction as passive dependents and their drive towards autonomy and citizenship.

Terry Goldie's analysis of Native Canadian cultural production has suggested that "the indigene as cultural item is similarly a result of hegemonic textualization."[22] Goldie's argument ends with selfhood: "If self can be viewed as collective, as manifest nation, then the indigene at present is most assuredly not-self, politically, economically, ideologically."[23] The corollary, converse insight also seems to be true: it is the lifting of legal and economic constraints, and the recognition of restitution claims in formerly colonized countries, that empower new forms of self-perception.

Nancy Rose Hunt outlines some of the shifts that have affected the explanatory paradigms of gender and history. The seventies revolution in authorship and subject matter introduced the social agency of African women. Next a "colonialism and culture" school examined gender meanings in colonial domesticity, reproduction, sexuality and the body. More recently both fiction and criticism have foregrounded issues of masculinity, subjective and social identities, generational and homo-social struggles. In South Africa Mark Behr's *The Smell of Apples* marks the last phase, linking sexual and political, private and public offensiveness, and the construction of gender codes in the apartheid state.

This analytical paradigm could be well applied to male African authors from Achebe to Farah, with both placing father-son conflicts on the agenda, but with Farah drawing attention, in *Sweet and Sour*

Milk to two temporal codes: the cyclical suffering of circumcised Somali women and the sudden deaths of political rebels, and Achebe using more traditional beliefs, myths and rituals, to highlight African precolonial structures and gender codes. Farah's work shows the impact of feminist thought, as does Achebe's later fiction, such as *Anthills of the Savannah* (1988)

In postcolonial and gender debates, influenced by cultural studies and deconstruction, there has been a movement from individual authorship to textuality, from roles and agency to oral history, identities, subjectivity, memory. Gender is seen as a set of social and symbolic relations. Representation, transnationalism, cultural production and everyday consumer culture are on the agenda. In Africa the critique of reified dualities has led to questions of how the colonized remade their relationships with one another, how they transformed social identities or dealt with the complexity of local conflicts at the core of social action. Bessie Head's volume of short stories, *The Collector of Treasures* (1977) is an illuminating example of a community dealing with sets of complex social relations in a rural African community at the time of decolonization. Such works demonstrate how African history was often made outside the colonial purview. Theoretical resistance paradigms have also begun to seem too simple when culture and politics are perceived as intertwined. With some accommodations between foreign and local elites after decolonization, Africans become and are perceived as consumers of capitalist culture. With the deconstructive view of the inevitable narrativization of history, some of the differences between fiction and non-fiction are broken down, and media, advertising, public and visual cultures can be read as social text, and for their explicit and implicit power relations.

Julia Emberley's thorough Canadian study, *Feminist Critique, Native Women's Writings, Postcolonial Theory* (1993), argues that "postcolonialism has shifted the critique of colonialism from strictly economic and political determinations to ideological ones."[24] Ideological mixing has created a site of hybridity which has also become a site of resistance on the part of indigenous peoples. Yet she goes on to say that "ideology functions in support of economic and political institutions to maintain the relations of domination and exploitation "between colonizer and colonized."[25] She also questions whether the paradigms of ethnicity and internal colonialism are sufficient to explain the continued marginalization of native peoples in Canada.[26] In her conclusions, and materialist feminist viewpoint, the textual collisions of sign systems are traceable to "conflicting relations between gatherer/hunter and capitalist modes of production."[27] She argues that the hierarchical value system of Western capitalism does not exist for hunter\gatherer societies, which create a different cognitive mapping of gender relations. This seems to overlook the different forms of distinction introduced by urbanization, education, and insider/outsider patterns, all of them gendered, and all part of the legacy of colonialism. To call the indigenous Canadian people a hunter/ gatherer society is partly to aboriginalize them, to homogenize and authenticate them in archaic time. African "womanism" has instead pointed to the limited institutional power of black men, the vocal responses of African women, and a shared anti-colonial struggle, as the reasons for less hierarchical and conflicted gender relations in Afro-American or aboriginal culture.

Rinaldo Walcott's stimulating work on racism and multiculturalism in Canada, and on fictions of Canadian identity, separates the oppression of immigrant minorities from aboriginal peoples, and the latter are excluded from the category of 'blackness'. Because 'blackness' is set up to fill a gap in the Canadian imaginary, it draws on diasporic theory and definitions, and could be seen as an extension or adaptation of transnational Negritude to Canadian conditions and to late capitalism. This paradigm seems to belong to Fanon's definition of racialized thought, though Walcott pursues his analysis into a variety of social material settings. The judicial system is discussed as a zone of conflict where racial definitions are contested, showing just how state-determined such conflicts are. Walcott's analysis is very useful in showing how " black allegiances to 'nation' are contingent upon the ethical practices of state administration and narratives of the nation,"[28] but his exclusion of First Nations peoples from 'blackness' seems to elide both the original complicity of racism and colonialism in Canada, and the more material land appropriations and claims which cannot and should not be elided in a theoretical model of nomadicism and migrancy. Borders are still policed; legal and territorial claims still have material histories and effects.

Arun Mukherjee's work on oppositional aesthetics draws attention to the knowledge/power intersections in teaching, academic institutions, and public structures. Her readings of minority writers and more particularly the historical and fictional relationships between India and Africa provide much material for comparative analysis. Her discussion of M.G. Vassanji's fiction points out the history of intracommunity politics, religious and social filiations, and internal tensions between minorities or oppressed groups. A comparison of Vassanji's portraits of everyday trading and familial relations in Tanzania with Ngugi wa Thiong'o's romantic nationalism in *A Grain of Wheat* highlights both migrant histories from East Africa and the everyday complicities of comprador groups which narratives of nationalism conceal. This discussion helps to break down the homogenized "native" voice which postcolonial critique sometimes suggests is recoverable in the authentically African voices of canonized writers such as Achebe, Soyinka and Armah.[29] This canon is male dominated, and women writers, such as Ama Ata Aidoo, Buchi Emecheta, and Tsitsi Dangerembga are often treated separately, which helps to affirm their sub-status. Florence Stratton has recently suggested that there is a dialogue going on between male and female African authors, but the history of African and colonial patriarchies is still so intertwined that not enough is said of the sexism of much African writing and its relation to colonial oppressions and cultural traditions.

It may be that postcolonial and gender theory have to take more account of research into linguistics itself, as language has such a complex power, especially in narrative forms of some duration which have developed under the historical conditions of Western education and decolonization. This is certainly the direction in which much of postmodern theory seems to point. Noam Chomsky discusses the theory of language as the mirror of the mind, and the links between language and cognitive psychology. He comments that "intrinsic to human nature is the desire to create under conditions of freedom and lack of constraint."[30] If such characteristics are at the core of human nature, "then any design of a just and decent society will have to accommodate to them."[31] He also points out that the media operate as a very distorted mirror of society because they "present and interpret social reality within a framework that is very largely set by domestic power."[32] This means the corporate system, the state executive and an extensive ideological system. The enclosures and dispossessions of European colonialism have had long-lasting effects on colonizers and colonized, both voluntary and involuntary, and it seems to be only in the relatively free exercise of the creative power of language, which harnesses profound unconscious power, that we can offer and be offered illuminating parables of the postcolonial condition.

What African literature has to teach us is that daily struggles for survival, for food and the labour or exchange systems which bring food into the home, are at the base of colonial and anti-colonial processes. It also teaches us of the power of dreaming, an ability to let many lives flow through our consciousness so that individuals and communities can flourish. The spiritual and mundane worlds are constantly interacting in an African metaphysic.

The night filled the room and swept over us, filling our space with light spirits, the old forms of animals; extinct birds stood near Dad's boots, a beautiful beast with proud eyes and whose hide quivered with gold-dust stood over the sleeping forms of Mum and Dad. A tree defined itself over the bed where I lay. It was an ancient tree, its trunk was blue, the spirit sap flowed in many brilliant colours up its branches, densities of light shone from its leaves. I lay horizontal in its trunk. The darkness moved; future forms, extinct tribes, walked through our landscape. They travelled new roads. They travelled for three hundred years and arrived in our night space. I did not have to dream. It was the first time I realized that an invisible space had entered my mind and dissolved part of the interior structure of my being. The wind of several lives blew into my eyes. The lives stretched far back and when I saw the great king of the spirit-world staring at me through the open doors of my eyes I knew that many things were calling me. It is probably because we have so many things in us that community is so important. The night was a messenger. In the morning I woke early and saw one of its messages on the floor. Mum and Dad, entwined, were still asleep. There were long tear-tracks on Mum's face. I slept again and when I woke the sun was warm, Dad's boots were gone, and Mum had left an orange for me on the table.

– (Ben Okri *The Famished Road* 445-6).

Notes

1. Larson 7.
2. Ibid 114.
3. Ibid 61.
4. Ibid 160.
5. Darby 136.
6. Ibid.
7. McClintock 353.
8. Darby 143.
9. Ibid 151.
10. Davidson 12.
11. Ibid 39.
12. Tutuola 302.
13. Okri 282.
14. Ibid.
15. Ibid 487.
16. Davidson 287.
17. Darby 164.
18. Fanon 130.
19. Ibid.
20. Fanon 212.
21. Fanon 212-213.
22. Goldie 216.
23. Ibid 222.
24. Emberley 6.
25. Ibid 7.
26. Ibid 18.
27. Ibid 25.
28. Walcott 92.
29. Mukherjee 170.
30. Chomsky 245.
31. Ibid.
32. Ibid.

Interview with Ellen Kuzwayo
Johannesburg, 15 May, 1986

Ellen Kate Cholofelo Nnoseng Motlalepulei Merafe was born in 1914, in Thaba Patchoa in the Orange Free State district of Thaba 'Nchu (the many names came from her grandparents on both sides). Her grandfather, Jeremiah Makgothi, was a trained teacher, a devout Christian, and secretary of the Native National Congress (later the ANC). Ellen Kuzwayo followed in his footsteps as a politically committed Christian.

She grew up on a large farm owned by her family which was taken from them by government legislation in 1974. She attended St Paul's Higher Primary School in Thaba'Nchu, and St Francis College, Mariannhill, Natal. She trained as a teacher at Adams College, Durban, and later at Lovedale College. After her marriage in 1941, she lived in Rustenburg, and bore two sons. The breakdown of her marriage led to a move to Johannesburg, where she became secretary of the Youth League of the ANC (1946). She married Godfrey Kuzwayo in 1950. She trained as a social worker (with Winnie Mandela) at the Jan Hofmeyr School of Social Work. Her social work has involved working for the YWCA and the School of Social Work at the University of the Witwatersrand. After the clashes of Soweto 1976 she became a member of the Committee of Ten, and a founder Board member of the Urban Foundation. In 1977/8 she was detained for five months at the Johannesburg Fort, but was released without being charged.

Kuzwayo's autobiography, *Call Me Woman* (1985) tells the story of her life as a member of a "privileged", Christian, land-owning family, a life which inevitably became intertwined with the political history of South Africa, with its legacy of Acts depriving blacks of their land, family rights, and political voice. The book is a lucid political and social document as well as a history of one woman's life.

I interviewed Ellen Kuzwayo in the downtown office of the Black Consumer Union in Johannesburg. Before the interview we spoke about Bessie Head's recent death, which had shocked her by its suddenness. The interview, which was more like a conversation than a formal interview, was conducted with us both speaking loudly into my son's "ghetto-blaster", lavishly decorated with African beads. Kuzwayo is an expressive and volatile speaker, with great sincerity. She has subsequently declared an interest in moving into the writing of fiction.

AC: What made you write *Call Me Woman*? What was the motive or idea behind it?

EK: The idea was to share my experiences in my practice as a social worker with as many people as possible – the experiences of black women I worked with during a period of about 12 years from 1963 to 1976. This was the real motive for writing the book. I tried to give a record of the lives of black women and the contributions they made to the development of this country, which people just close their eyes to.

AC: So it was really in support of all the women that you worked with. Do you feel quite strongly that you're representing a broader group in the country?

EK: I feel so, particularly a group that has been disadvantaged for as long as South Africa has been here: people who have been the underdogs of this country, who have been suppressed and looked down upon. And I felt people did not know who they were and the contribution they've made in this country.

AC: Yes, I noticed that you often thanked people and mentioned specific names. You say that it is because black women have been silent that they haven't had their contribution acknowledged, and seem to suggest sometimes that authorship is a way of giving people a voice?

EK: That's right!

AC: Do you think they've been ignored or silent because they've been living in an oral culture, not a written culture?

EK; No, not that so much. I think the present history could have given them an opportunity to do so, but they have been the underdogs, the lowest in the society, primarily because they were not given the same opportunity to start when the men started an education. And in industry, too, when they eventually got in, because they did not study a good time in their education, they were also disadvantaged. They were the people who remained with the children and the old people at home. At some time they dared to come into the cities, and when they got into the cities, they could – only a few of them, a very small percentage – fit into domestic work. Some of them, because of lack of schooling, could not communicate with the people who wanted to employ them. This was a real hurdle. They also found the life in the towns quite foreign. And that is why I wrote about those who took to beer-making, because that was an industry to them. Some of them did a little bit of work as charwomen- coming to the house and doing washing and cleaning. But by and large they could not properly integrate into industry, because of lack of education and their being unable to communicate with those who employed them. But, when looking deep into what they did out there, when their husbands were in the cities, and they had little income, one can see that they managed to keep the adults, the old people, the sickly, the youngsters, together. And they tried to get into the fields to make ends meet because their husband's salaries or wages were so very low.

AC: So you see them as having great strengths for survival and strategies for coping?

EK: And how! And how! The support systems in the black community played a tremendous role, because when the husbands were here, with no exception in all black groups, no matter what language they speak, people had the ability to support one another. And one major thing that is common in all black communities is the "work camp" system, called-in one language or another – "ntsima" in Tswana and Sesotho, and "ilima" in Zulu and Nguni language. These are support systems in "work camps" where I, if I wanted my field to be hoed, would go out and announce it – or my husband would probably go and announce it – and I would prepare the meals for that day, when everybody would come and hoe my field. This hoeing we did together: we work together, we act together. And at the end of the day it was great joy for people to come together and just sing and celebrate. It was a feature that was real in all black communities in rural areas, and it is still real to this day where people have patches of land. But the only feeling now is that perhaps there is not sufficient food, people can't make the beer that they want to make, people don't have enough variety of produce to slaughter and cook a meal, and to entertain the people that are there for the day.

AC: There are special social and psychological problems for black women, and those have intensified with the conflict being centred in a younger generation now. Would you say that the role of women has changed a lot in South Africa in recent years? Is there a split between mothers and children, or have those older women, perhaps more conservative women, been radicalised? You say in your book that perhaps your attitude has changed towards things like theft because of the political situation. Would you say that is general?

EK: I don't want to go that far. But I personalize this, because I felt it was something that other people would probably not be aware of. I have gradually been made aware of this: you know, when you have a very strong negative feeling about something, and then suddenly you begin to wonder why you condemn it, and I have gone beyond condemning. I sympathize with these kids and I say, For goodness sake, they have been traumatized. They can't go into the cities like other children, and look for jobs. If they do, the police get at them, and they send them to some unknown country which is said to be a homeland for them. And because of this trauma, kids have gone underground. They have become something else; they are no longer the children that they were in the 1950s. They have sought ways of protecting themselves in the process. And this protection has mingled with other things. When you are not working, you'll find a means for surviving and some of their means, their ways and strategies of surviving, are not acceptable in society. Some of them end up stealing, breaking into shops and taking people's money. And you say, really, who is at fault here? Is it the children? Is it the system? If white children were placed in the same situation, would they probably not react the same way? Is it because these children are bad as children, or is it because they are forced to do the things that they are doing, because of the system in the country? And in the long run, you who are the mother, something turns inside you; and I think, for goodness sake, if they get away with something, I pray to God that they are never discovered. But like children they get so excited and they show off. I would never, at the moment, bow down to take property which is not mine. And yet at the same time, I sympathize with these children, because they find themselves in a situation that probably they never contemplated at any time.

AC: Would you say your own experience within your family has played a role there, your son's experiences, and the fact that you've seen your own children suffer?

EK: My children have not gone that way. They have struggled. If they are not working they are not working, then fine. I know my eldest son is not working, but the fact that he can do accounts helps; he has no regular job but he can go and at least find a way. If I compare them – a thing that I did not want to do- somehow they have emerged without tarnish in terms of theft and other things. But when my children were very young – at the ages of 2 and 4 – the Children's Act did not cover them or make me free to bring them here from Rustenburg.

AC: Yes, there was that separation...

EK: The separation – and at a time when white children could easily have gone with their mothers. But because mine were black, and they were born in Rustenburg, they could not come into Johannesburg. It is a tremendous frustration, and to that extent I identify with other mothers; but thank God, they never went astray. My three boys, you know, they are all married. They keep to their homes and they don't go out at night to go catching on people, and stealing people's things. I am a social worker by profession, and as such I worked some time with youth, and they used to share with me their frustrations. I think that sharing was important, but suddenly I see this radical change, children behaving differently. Whereas during the time I was practising with them as a social worker they were a different lot of children.

AC: You seem to have a special feeling for children and sympathy with young people. Reading between the lines: your own experience of childhood, were there certain hurtful things?

EK: That's right.

AC: And there seems to me to be a connection between your sense of being slightly different or left out in some way at some time, and your extra sympathy with young people?

EK: I lived in two worlds, you know. I was very protected in my early days as a child with my grandparents on that farm. I was very well cared for and as a child I had fantasies about life. I know I had great expectations which probably finally were not fulfilled, or if they were fulfilled, instead of getting the joys of life that I anticipated, I sometimes got rude shocks: in my first marriage for one thing. And as a child, when I was turned out because my mother and father divorced, I wasn't aware of the reasons. You know how you live a very protected life and you assume that certain things are really right with you, and then suddenly someone says, "Look, you don't belong. You don't belong, get out!"

AC: There was the shock of that?

EK: That was a very big shock in my life. But because it was within the family, it was not a system thing.

AC: That's different from the kind of experience, say, of a bad marriage that you, because you are a black woman, can't get out of...

EK: Exactly!

AC: ...or you can't be with your children because there is a law prohibiting you.

EK: That marriage, true, I could get out of it. It was at a time when I could say, For goodness' sake, what am I sitting here for? My children might have been a reason for me to stay. The only other thing I had to say, if I stay on here, is that I may go mad or die. And these kids that I am trying to stand for will miss me. Is it not better for me to go and live for them somewhere?

AC: It was a difficult choice to make.

EK: It was a very difficult choice to make. But the black women in this country have had a raw deal at every point. You know, because they were women and there was this culture that discriminated against them- particularly if you had not had an education, you thought, Well, I've got to take it. I have no choice. On the other hand if you had education you thought, Why am I sitting here? You begin to question so many things. And in the process you say, I don't think this is the type of thing that I can kill myself for.

AC: Would you say that African women, then, suffered in the way you did, say, in your first marriage, because black men have been raised to believe that they have a special right to treat their wives in certain ways, according to traditional custom?

EK: Yes. I think, first and foremost, men by and large anywhere in the world see themselves as superior to women. Why? And the culture thing is added on to this.

AC: It intensifies it?

EK: It intensifies it; and the fact that black men first had an opportunity to first go to school and get into industry added on to this.

AC: The first to urbanize?

EK: They were open to urbanization much earlier than their womenfolk. And this intensified the gap and it also intensified the pressure on the black women. They were always left out, swept aside, and that is why I admire their achievement in education, particularly in fields that were always seen as exclusively for men and for women of other communities than black women, I think they have done very well. And when you come to think of the fact that black women went into medicine in the forties, very late, in '47 the first black woman doctor emerged. And in 1967, twenty years after, the first black woman lawyer emerged.

AC: Yes, I see you list those achievements in your book. They are very special.

EK: Yes, they are, because when you come to think of the conditions, first and foremost just at home, how they had to struggle to get out of that, to say, "I'm going to make it." And always being told, you know, in school, "Women can't make it!" And when there were science classes, women were always expected to go and do domestic science, something lower, because they were not capable. And the first woman who dared was so capable that she became an inspiration to others. And after that you can see the numbers grow. I tried to analyze some of them, but not in the book.

AC: But you do mention in the book a number of women who seem to have been role models, or inspirations. Because it is very useful for women who are deprived to see that somebody can do it, and that is an encouragement to all.

EK: Yes, yes.

AC: I want to ask you about the actual writing of the book, because what interests me is this process of writing, and why. Black women don't often commit themselves to print. Do you think that has a special value for women, to communicate through print?

EK: I think it is very important. I have an aunt – she's still alive, she's 86 now – and, you know, I was staggered. I was already doing the research then, for my book. And I went to my aunt (who is my mother's youngest sister and was a nursing sister as well as a midwife) because I wanted to get certain facts straight from her about the family. And to my great surprise, she knelt down (she didn't even ask me to kneel down), and pulled this little suitcase from somewhere. And she opened it and she said, "Look, I've got these three documents here". She had committed herself at that age to writing. She had written about her father.

AC: That is extraordinary. I remember now: you mention in the book finding these things.

EK: Exactly. She had written these records about her father, about the history of how the black people (the Tswana people) got to Thaba'Nchu. And she had written about herself – she always said this — she said, "This is my obituary". I said, "Why did you write your own obituary?" She said, "I feel I must write, because I have been to funerals where false things have been said about people. A cousin of mine was said to have been overseas, and he had never been there. So I don't want people to say things that are not right about me."

AC: So it was to put the record straight and to give the correct information?

EK: Exactly.

AC: But it must have been very unusual to do that at the time.

EK: I was very inspired-I mean it was in the subconscious when I went away. She had these papers and she has them now. She is still alive and she keeps on reminding me that when she dies people will make no mistake: "Here is my obituary". And then, what interested me more was that when I went to ask a friend at Fort Hare to find out if there were any records at the archives at Lovedale about my grandfather (her father) – things that he had said- she said that all the archives at Lovedale had been moved into Fort Hare, because the government had turned Lovedale into something else. And when I got that write-up about my grandfather and compared it with what my aunt had said I found it almost the same, except that the archives were much more detailed. But in general my aunt was right, even about the history of a political split in the radicals. And I've been asking myself, How many black people would do that?

I'll tell you why I took so long to write (and I think this is the problem with many people): we are paid so little in the jobs that we do that for the greater part of our lives we are struggling to survive. For a long time I wanted to write this book, but I had to decide whether to abandon my job and starve and write. This is the problem of many black writers, not only women. A friend of my father's, Mr Skota, after whom Skotaville [publishing house] is named, was a black man who lived in Bloemfontein and wrote the first "Who's who in the black community". If you saw him you'd weep. You could see that here was a very intelligent man. But because the income on which he lived was so very little he could not really give time to those things that he wanted to do. And finally I said: "Ellen Kuzwayo, If I live on the side my bread is buttered, I'll never write this book". So I chucked the job.

AC: Did you get a grant to write the book?

EK: I came to Johannesburg and knocked at somebody's door, and said: "Please, sponsor me in writing a book". And he gave me that sponsorship for two years – for three years actually, but after two years it was the end of the road. And when I went overseas to look for a publisher, and some people saw what I had done, somebody overseas in Liverpool said, "I'm prepared to help you so that you can finish at the end of the year". That helped me. And I can imagine that there are many people with a great talent for writing, but because all the time they are nursing this meagre wage, few of them have time to write.

AC: Pure economic restriction, that's what it is?

EK: Because of the political structure of this country.

AC: And did you find the actual process of writing difficult? Or did it come readily?

EK: I enjoyed it. And I never sat and talked into a machine like this. I write, it comes through here, it comes onto my pen, onto my paper. This is how I write. [Runs her hand down the side of her head, over her shoulder, and down her arm, to her fingers, then claps her hands.)

AC: You didn't do much rewriting?

EK: Oh, yes!

AC: So you did a lot of rewriting? But you got the initial thing down?

EK: Exactly. I got it down. And the rewriting really came with the editing, when they were changing one portion – let's say, the sequence. That bogged me down. I could cry about that; the editing of any book that is going to come out is trying. I know when I was in London I sometimes used to get up in the morning, go to bed in the afternoon, get up again at eleven at night and sleep at four in the morning. Just rewriting and putting material in sequence. But the actual writing of that initial thing-it just came. I enjoyed it. I loved it. I woke up with everybody in the morning, had my bath, took my bag, got into my car. Eight-thirty I was at varsity, where they gave me an office, and I sat in that office and shut myself off from everybody until four o'clock or four-thirty in the afternoon. I just told myself that somebody has given me money and I've got to use it profitably, and therefore this is a job for me. There's nobody who says, "Go to work". But I must tell myself, I've got to do this job.

AC: And are you happy with what finally emerged in your book?

EK: Yes.

AC: It reads very clearly. Did you participate in the editing with somebody else? You didn't subject yourself to somebody who would do things that you didn't like? Because I think sometimes it happens that a white editor steps in?

EK: Now when that happened, particularly when I was overseas, I had to say at some point, "Stop! That and that and that and that is coming back into it."

AC: So your collaboration was there all the time? Otherwise it might have been changed too much?

EK: Exactly. You know it's amazing: when you write your first book you are almost over-trusting. You think that the people who are helping you, have... I think they do have your welfare at heart. Let me give them that. But I think sometimes that they don't know what you want in the book. And if you are not careful people are going to put into your book things they think are worthwhile, and push out the things you think are worthwhile.

AC: Do you think that you feel any special sympathy with other writers in South Africa or outside? We were talking about Bessie Head earlier, and I see she writes a very sympathetic Preface to your book. Have you read a lot of fiction, autobiography, biography or did you work more from your experience?

EK: I had read a lot here. Very early in my life I read Mary O'Reilly, who used to write fiction. She wrote a lot of books and I read a lot of that stuff at a very early age. Then later on I started reading for reading's sake. And I enjoyed it. Except perhaps for books that I had read at school – you know prescribed books can make you sick sometimes [Laughter]. It's not like the literature that you pick up in a library for your own interest. And I read a great deal of this, but strangely enough at that time it never said to me, "Write something!"

I also used to sit down and do a lot of sketching. Mountain scenery and so on, but I threw everything away. I still have that itch to this day. If I sit in a meeting, at the end of that meeting I've put sketches on paper, but it's not anything that is mature, say like the book I have written. And maybe it's because I don't understand the implications of sketching. Then drawing fell away. I became more interested in language. I've always been able to speak — address meetings, large groups of people.

AC: How do you respond to other women writers?

EK: I'm enjoying reading black American women writers. I think Miriam Tlali has done good work inside the country and should be acclaimed as a black woman writer. But she hasn't had the acknowledgement she deserves. This causes frustration.

AC: Would you choose a black publisher in preference to a white?

EK: Possibly I would, because of the political situation, I was afraid that my book might be banned because of my experiences and my detention. So I thought it would be better to find a publisher outside South Africa.

AC: What sort of audience did you have in mind for your book?

EK: I wanted a South African audience, more than any other, but there was the fear of banning. I was aiming at the white South African readership, to tell them what a black woman thinks, and how she lives. But I thought they would be able to find the book overseas. Whites are wealthy, and they travel a lot.

AC: What are your plans for the future? Would you consider writing a novel?

EK: I don't think I would do well in fiction. I would want to write about aspects of my own community. I've just done a piece for a magazine (*Leadership*) on migrant labour. I'm a social worker.

AC: So you see your job as social worker as crucial to your writing?

EK: Yes. Very much so. I'm pleased that I changed my job from teaching to social work. There are too many limitations on teachers in this country. There are still limitations in social work, make no mistake, but fewer than in the teaching profession. My life as a social worker widened my horizons. It is easier to serve your community in that way. My aim is to serve my community.

Interview with Obi Maduakor
University of Guelph, December 16, 1998

AC: Fanon argues that national liberation is the "material keystone" which makes a national culture possible. In the West African fiction you've been teaching in your course at Guelph, on post-independence disillusionment in postcolonial African fiction, the problems of political instability and inequity are central. Is national liberation in West African countries a myth?

OM: I think I see national liberation as a myth. The problems we have in Africa now are related to poverty and ignorance. We talk about democracy; we want practical democracy, but this is undermined by two main factors. The first is the instrument that could bring about democracy: elections are rigged and voters are intimidated. Those in power are not truly chosen by the people, but are those who are able to buy their way through or intimidate voters; so even under a civilian government we can't claim to have a true democracy. Secondly, practical democracy is also undermined by the influence of the military. They can seize power at any time. Writers may want to or may believe they can influence political action, but the people are simply too hungry to fight for freedom or independence. As long as poverty and ignorance exist in Africa, as long as the masses are hungry, national liberation remains a myth.

AC: In the post-independence period, have the military coups in any way been a stimulus to protest writing?

OM: It has given some incentive to writing, but though there is a school of radical writers, they are unable to bring about change, because of the problems I've just mentioned. People can talk and talk as much as they like but it has little effect. The military is powerful, and the rich civilians, the political elite, have a lot of influence, and can intimidate the people and stay in power for as long as they wish.

AC: Is there such a thing as an African aesthetic? Do you define it in terms of the African past, of traditional pre-colonial culture, or in terms of what African literature has achieved to date, because African writing has evolved?

OM: I have two views on African aesthetics. One concerns the African worldview where, in African aesthetics, reality cannot be compartmentalized. Reality comprises what is real and what is sur-real. The supernatural and real worlds form part of a total worldview, so that you cannot divorce African aesthetics from this worldview. Some writers move between these two worlds, the real world and the supernatural, for example Ben Okri and the Ghanaian writer, Kofi Awoonor. So we cannot divorce our concern with the known from the unknown, the religious and the supernatural.

In terms of what we've achieved nowadays, African aesthetics concerns committed literature. If you're writing African literature, you must have a purpose. Writing in Africa is geared to political liberation. Achebe says the writer is a teacher, has something to communicate to the community. He's not just writing for pleasure. Those are my two views: real and supernatural worlds, and a sense of committed literature.

AC: One of the reasons I ask is that in South Africa there is a long tradition of commitment to political struggle, but when people talk of an African aesthetic they often mean only black African writers, Black Consciousness, but the committed tradition you speak of is found in South African white writers as well.

OM: I mean Africa as a whole: South, East and West Africa. African literature is very much a committed literature, in terms of political liberation.

AC: How do you see the relationship between African fiction and history? Has West African historiography been much influenced by independence? In South Africa a Eurocentric view dominated the writing of history for so long, and a revisionist historiography emerged in reaction. Has history been conceptualized from the point of view of the oppressed, in Nigeria or elsewhere?

OM: What gives literature validity in Nigeria and Africa generally is history. There is this interface between literature and history.

Achebe's first novel, *Things Fall Apart*, is based on colonial history; he wants to re-write African history to show that Africans had a rich civilization in the past. So literature has been strongly influenced by history. What is happening in society, the political direction, political corruption, is also giving impetus to fiction. There is a symbiotic relationship between fiction and history. Fiction takes its cue from history and develops from there: condemning history, re-writing history, and showing how history has been badly written, trying to put it in a proper perspective. Even corruption is part of social history, and literature reflects this situation as well.

AC: Which historians have been important to you in conceptualizing colonial viewpoints?

OM: We have a great historian, Professor Adiele Afigbo. He is Igbo, so he goes back to Igbo history, shows Igbo background and history and re-writes the Igbo history that was truncated by colonial misrepresentations.

AC: That's a form of cultural retrieval?

OM: Yes, but I think literature does it even better than history, as we see in the case of Achebe.

AC: Would you say exile, imprisonment, and censorship have been major factors affecting the production, continuity and reception of West African fiction? Are there differences here between countries and regions?

OM: Of course, if a writer is imprisoned he cannot create. Ken Saro-Wiwa was a great writer in Nigeria. When he was in prison he could not write. Some writers are hindered by fear of censorship. So these two factors do hinder the production of literature to a very great extent. In terms of exile, it depends upon the reason why the writer is in exile. If he's in exile voluntarily, he may still be able to write great literature, like James Joyce who exiled himself from Ireland, but was still able to write great literature about Ireland. A number of southern African writers are in exile: Lewis Nkosi and Dennis Brutus are able to write even better because they have a nostalgia for their beloved country. Now Achebe is in exile, living in America; and Kofi Awoonor was a diplomat away from Ghana for many years, but imaginatively he was always returning to his country. So exile may not hinder creativity very much if it is voluntary exile. Even in involuntary exile, if a writer is free and truly aware of where he is, he may still be able to return imaginatively and write great literature.

AC: I can't think of many African writers who have gone into exile and changed their subject, their country of imaginative focus. This is less true of South Africa; one thinks of Dan Jacobson and Doris Lessing, even the late Peter Abrahams. But West and East African writers who live outside Africa still write about it; there's a strong commitment.

OM: Yes, but they're rooted to their background. If you want to write a good work of literature, you write best about what you know best. You may live in Europe for many years, but if you're not integrated into the culture you will not be able to produce good work. Even Ben Okri, who lives in London, goes back imaginatively to Africa, to Nigeria.

AC: It's fine if you can go back, but in some South African cases people left on exit permits, or they were frightened of returning because of the risk of reimprisonment. That seems to have been the case in West Africa sometimes too.

OM: No, we don't have that kind of fear in West Africa. You're thinking of South Africa, where writers were very afraid to return under the apartheid regime.

AC: What about writers who have been imprisoned in West Africa?

OM: Soyinka was in prison for about a year. Kofi Awoonor was in prison for about a year. They were able to write some poetry in prison. It wasn't a longstanding imprisonment.

AC: But it would create a fear of a repetition?

OM: Yes, it does. Actually, Soyinka is in exile now, but now that we have a military government that is not very dictatorial, he went home to Nigeria about a month ago and was given a hero's welcome. So if one is in prison, there's a problem, there's a hindrance to creative imagination, but if it doesn't last for too long you can be released and go on with your creative endeavour. And of course the experience can become the subject matter of literature as well.

AC: That's certainly been the case in South Africa. How about censorship? I'm thinking of the reception of works. There are so many factors that already separate the writer from the mass of readership – has censorship been a limiting factor as well?

OM: In West Africa the press has generally been free. Writers can say almost anything they like except that they cannot abuse leaders personally. You can criticise them. In Nigeria the press is quite free.

AC: And how about novels, and non-fiction?

OM: There is a book of poems by Odia Ofeimun, *The Poet Lied*, which is critical of Nigerian leaders, but these poems are still published. We don't have much censorship in West Africa as such.

AC: In the fictional world there is a lot of lively political debate. Nigeria is obviously a very dynamic culture in that way. Ordinary people are always discussing politics, and that gets into the literature.

OM: Yes, political debate is vigorous. It was only Abacha who was rather too strict with writers, but even then the press was free. Although he did imprison some journalists who attacked him personally. Apart from that, writers and the press are free in West Africa.

AC: What would you say have been the main effects on culture and literature of the political instability in Africa, especially the coups and counter-coups of Nigeria? I'm thinking of South Africa where it has been argued that political oppression enforced certain genres on black writers, such as poetry and the short sketch, as opposed to forms like the novel which need privacy and time. One thinks of Ngugi's use of the theatre, and taking theatre to the people.

OM: Yes, we do have popular drama in Nigeria, and also popular fiction. The situation is that instability does give writers an opportunity to express themselves. It stimulates art, although Achebe was rather silent for about twenty years after his fourth novel. In 1987, when he published *Anthills of the Savannah*, he eventually broke this silence and wrote a great work. Before that he was disappointed with events: the civil war and the general instability. That locked up his imagination; he couldn't write for twenty years, but when he did write again he produced something very great. There are thus two effects: instability may stimulate a writer; it can also frustrate a writer in some ways.

AC: As you say, it can produce popular literature, because people are angry and debating. There's the Onitsha market literature in Nigeria.

OM: And also what we call guerrilla theatre. Its intention is to take the target of the satire by surprise.

AC: What about involving people in traditional rituals, theatre and masquerade? It seems to be one effect of oppression that people re-activate traditions. I'm thinking of Soyinka's plays.

OM: Yes, Soyinka uses several theatrical idioms, including ritual, to disguise his message.

AC: Simon Gikandi has asked how African intellectuals "can extend their experiences to those excluded from powers and privileges ushered in by independence, and how can they develop a fundamental knowledge about the conditions of a populace so different from them"? What do you think? Which writers have been most successful in doing this?

OM: In Nigeria the elites are still writing for elites. We have a group of writers who call themselves socialist realist writers who have wanted to reach the common people, but they still write in English and the common people are predominantly uneducated and illiterate. The best way a writer can reach out to the common people is to write in the language of the common man, to write in a vernacular language. In Nigeria this has not been the case. It is Ngugi who has reached out to the common people in Kenya by writing in Gikuyu. You can also reach them through drama and stage presentation: popular theatre or guerrilla theatre. But in terms of written work, the best way to reach a large audience is to write in their language. That's why Ngugi has been very popular in Kenya. But he does have a problem: he can't be read beyond Kenya except in translation. This is a problem for African writers who write in the vernacular: they then have to be translated into English, or French.

AC: Writing in South Africa in indigenous languages has tended to be taken up in the educational system and as a result has not been a very vibrant literature. Is there a flourishing literature in indigenous languages in West Africa?

OM: Yes, we have a lot of literature written in Yoruba, both poetry and drama. We do have some novels and plays in Igbo which are read in the schools. But Igbo intellectuals enjoy their facility in the English language. Now there is a movement for a return to roots, with writers drawing on rich vernacular idioms. We have departments of Igbo studies in many universities in Nigeria.

AC: Some critics say that it is in the novel that the West and Africa meet. What do you think are the key achievements of the African novel; can it be discussed separately from the rise of the novel in English literature?

OM: I would contest the idea that the novel is a Western genre. I think storytelling is universal. Africans have been telling and writing stories for a very long time, perhaps not on a very grand scale. It's not new. Writers are used to telling stories, so telling stories on a grand scale is just an adaptation. Achebe may have imitated Joseph Conrad – you can borrow the form from the West – but the idea of telling stories is fundamental to Africa.

AC: I was making a distinction between telling stories and the novel genre, because in Africa there's been an oral tradition for much longer, whereas the literate tradition, the writing of novels, is much more recent.

OM: In terms of literary tradition we do draw on Western conventions. We write realistic novels in the tradition of English novelists. But even though there's realism, we still introduce folktales, legends and rituals, and other forms of the oral tradition are also brought to bear upon the writing. And ancestor worship is very important. In Achebe's novels you have ancestor worship – return to ritual, evocation of the supernatural world of the dead – because in the world-view I mentioned earlier there is no demarcation between the world of the dead, the world of the unborn, and the world of the living – they're all inter-related. That's a new dimension to the Western tradition of the novel. It is not purely realistic; it's also surreal or even super-real. To that extent African novelists have adapted the genre of the Western novel.

AC: Writers like Ekwensi and Ike seem to have produced prolific popular fiction. How do you see the relationship between more intellectual novelists like Achebe and such popular fiction?

OM: Ike and Ekwensi have written a lot of popular fiction, but the problem is that those who created the canon are intellectuals, university dons, so there's a tendency to neglect popular writing in favour of highly intellectual fiction by Achebe, Soyinka and Armah. These are the books, by literary intellectual writers, that get studied in universities, perhaps in order to inculcate a sense of the literary in the students. Then there is the problem of art: Ekwensi is not very conscious of literary art. He has a well-made plot: people go to the city, and get contaminated. You have robbery, crime, prostitution. Eventually the hero gets converted and returns to the village as a reformed character. You can always predict the outcome of an Ekwensi novel. This predictability lessens the interest of the reader. Ike and Ekwensi are not interested in modernist experimentation in language and style. That's part of their problem.

AC: So it's formula writing?

OM: Yes, formulaic and populist. The target audience may be the common people. It's a development from the Onitsha popular tradition.

AC: I found the social problems were clearer.

OM: Yes, social problems of crime, what happens among schoolgirls and traders, among city-dwellers. It's not a refined literature that people want to teach in the universities. Those who established that canon have neglected such popular writing. But I believe the trend is changing.

AC: But do they have greater popular consumption, because people see their daily lives reflected in them?

OM: Yes, they do. But then, someone has to create the tradition, and this is done by university intellectuals who favour works written in the manner of the great tradition.

AC: Whose great tradition?

OM: Well, Achebe's great tradition. Achebe, Armah, Ngugi. There may be a change in direction, eventually. We may begin to look at the popular writers like Ike and Ekwensi; but the giants I mentioned are now on the throne.

AC: So in the universities only the main figures are taught?

OM: Yes, the first generation of writers. Those who started it all are very influential, because of their innovations in style and technique. There's also an intellectual background to their work. You have something to challenge you as you read them.

AC: There have been very different attitudes to the use of English in African fiction: from Sartre who saw it as a colonialist plot, to Aidoo who says English is a good vehicle to reach other African audiences and readerships, to Ngugi's politically motivated return to vernacular theatre and fiction. What is your view of this debate?

OM: We have a language problem in Africa. For example, in Nigeria there are over 500 languages. What language are you going to write in? We have Igbo, Yoruba, Hausa, and there are many other language groups. Not all are literate in the main languages either. Achebe makes this point in an interview. Even though it may be good to write in the vernacular, what about the other people you want to reach? The best thing is to use the language that unites us: English, the lingua franca. And with English you can reach every audience in Nigeria as well as abroad. But then you may domesticate English, as Achebe has done. It doesn't have to be Oxford English. It's the best compromise we can make. Even though Ngugi writes in Gikuyu, he still has to translate, because there are many other tribes, even in Kenya. So writing in the vernacular becomes a nationalistic gesture.

AC: There are very expressive local forms of English, like pidgin.

OM: Yes, there is pidgin, common people's language, and also transliteration of vernacular thoughts and rhythms and idioms. It's not standard English as such.

AC: Pidgin seems to convey so much of the cultural attitudes, social problems, and humour.

OM: Yes, it reaches out to everyone in the community.

AC: And it challenges the Western reader, who has to do some work to understand it.

OM: But the sense of pidgin is usually very clear from the context; the reader can usually decipher it. It's Ngugi who gives me lots of problems. When I read *Petals of Blood* and his use of Gikuyu there, I'm not able to decipher the meaning from the context, and he doesn't provide a glossary at the end.

AC: You've discussed in your course Achebe 's attempts to dismantle traditional attitudes towards women in his later fiction. Florence Stratton has pointed out that African authors have developed an intertextual dialogue about gender. Who have been the main African novelists contributing to the dismantling of gender inequities? Is homophobia a problem, given the stress on traditional masculine codes, separate spheres for men and women, and the colonial reinforcement of European family patterns? Is there an emergent gay literature?

OM: No, we don't have gay literature in Africa right now. Even feminist writers call themselves feminists with a small 'f. For Buchi Emecheta and other feminist writers marriage and family solidarity still have value. All they're asking for is that women be recognized for who they are: they are important members of the community and should be recognized for their talents. So in terms of gay writing, no, no, no. The society is still closely knit. Family is a very important structure in Africa. Even though African culture is strongly masculine, there is a dismantling of masculine egotism within the literature. As Stratton points out, there is now a literary dialogue around gender issues. Ngugi, in the portrayal of Wanja in *Petals of Blood*, has been able to dismantle this inequity; he shows that women have many talents, are very industrious, and should be respected. That is why in Wanja he creates a very important, intelligent, responsible character. Petals of Blood was published in 1977. And of course Achebe followed with *Anthills of the Savannah* in 1987, where we have Beatrice, an important, interesting character, very liberated. Even though Beatrice doesn't want marriage or family, she's not gay. As regards gay literature, Africans are very god-fearing and religious, so their religious sense prohibits sexual perversion.

AC: But homosexuality exists in Africa, and so does AIDS. Have these problems not stimulated any cultural expression?

OM: If AIDS exists in Africa, it's not spread through homosexuality. It may have spread through visitors. In East Africa there are a lot of tourists, and AIDS may have been a contamination from tourists in East Africa. This is what I really believe. Gay liberation is not very strong in Africa. It does not exist in Africa as such. Those who are homosexual go underground, and are in a minority. The society is still very homogeneous, very religious, and still honours family. It's not like Europe or America. Nor am I wishing for any kind of gay literature.

AC: There are forms of denigration in the literature though. In Ike's *The Search* there are contemptuous references to homosexuals. It seems to me related to the very strong masculine codes which are such a strong focus in Achebe's early work, for instance. Transactions between men, and male honour, take up a lot of space and provide motives for the action.

OM: No, no. If Ike is denigrating homosexuality, it is from a strong religious motivation. It's not a sign of a masculine culture or power. If he condemns it, it is because homosexuality is not approved religiously or socially. Also it's a strong taboo in our society and we pray it remains so.

AC: A while ago the critiques of European critics on African literature and culture, and of Eurocentric bias and patronage, were quite heated. In South Africa European critical writing on black authors has been the major form of criticism, and there have been few black critical voices. I notice that criticism of West African literature by Europeans has often taken an anthropological form, which can be divorced from aesthetic judgement. Is this still an important issue or are there now enough indigenous critical voices to make the issue less important?

OM: There's a lot of change now, because there are many intellectuals, university lecturers in Africa now. I want to return to that earlier debate: Who should be a critic of African literature? I think that anyone who has been trained in literature should be able to approach the literature of any region or community, once you've been trained to use the tools of literary criticism. After all, we read English literature, Shakespeare, Jane Austen, Joseph Conrad, and we should not be banned from writing criticism on the work of those writers because we're not English. The cultural background may not be very clear, the cultural nuances may be missed, but if you do research into those areas, you can grasp the connotations. So I don't think we should ban Western intellectuals from the criticism of African literature just because they're not Africans. It may work the other way around. Their critiques may influence us too, because we are literary scholars. They may have a problem in terms of background, but if they go to Africa and study the cultural background they may well be able to interpret the cultural relations in those works. Some of them had a problem initially. There are critics like Bernth Lindfors: he's not an African, yet he's one of the greatest critics of African literature. You cannot ban him from the critical arena. It's a matter of becoming familiar with the cultural background of the literature you're studying, as we ourselves became familiar with the English background of the writers we studied in university.

AC: David Carroll has suggested that the role of the African writer has shifted from historian to critic to social reformer. Do you agree?

OM: That's a cleverly devised description, and quite true. Achebe's evolution has certainly followed that paradigm. First he went to

African history in *Things Fall Apart* and gave validity to that history. Then he moved to *A Man of the People* where he criticizes the political elite in what has become a tradition of post-independence disillusionment. There he becomes a critic of his own people who have abused power. Then in *Anthills of the Savannah* he makes the case for social reform as against revolution. In revolution the old order is perpetuated, but the answer lies in reforming the psyche of the people through education. So David Carroll has described Achebe's own development from history to criticism to social reformation. But I would also talk of social reform in terms of socialist realism, the approach of radical Marxist writers who think they can bring about social change through a radical approach to writing. That is also part of reform. That's the direction novels in Africa are taking now.

AC: I was interested to see that in Achebe's trilogy he begins with traditional Igbo society, shows modern corruption and bribery in *No Longer at Ease*, and then returns to cultural tradition and religion in *Arrow of God*. The trilogy has that circular structure; he seems to say, after showing you the post-independence world, let me show you again what that cultural richness was.

OM: It would be interesting to find out if *Arrow of God* or *No Longer at Ease* was written first. I think that *Arrow of God* was written before *No Longer at Ease*, but *No Longer at Ease* was published first.

AC: Whatever the order of composition or publication, he chooses to put *Arrow of God* at the end of the trilogy.

OM: Yes, in terms of date of publication that's what he did. *Arrow of God* was published in 1964 or so.

AC: You think it was just a practical thing. I thought it also had a poetic and cultural function. You move as a reader through colonial and post-independence problems and then you are returned to spiritual traditions. This structure seemed to me to have a healing function, and to be circular.

I'd like to move on now to generational differences. There's now an established international set of renowned African writers like Achebe, Ngugi, and Soyinka. What differences do you see in the second generation of African novelists, such as Ben Okri?

OM: When I speak of socialist realism, I'm talking of second-generation writers. They believe the first generation of writers did not go far enough in making a change. They simply condemned events. They didn't offer solutions as to how the situation could be improved. They accused the Achebe of *A Man of the People*, the Soyinka of *The Interpreters*, the Armah of *Fragments* and *The Beautyful Ones Are Not Yet Born* of not going far enough. These earlier writers highlighted the ills of society but stopped at critical realism; they offered no solutions or directions for improvement. The second-generation writers are Marxist-oriented, very radical. They are oriented toward social change. Who are they? Kole Omotoso, Femi Osofisan, Bode Sowande, Odia Ofeimun, Festus Iyayi. These are the younger writers who are radical and socialist. They admire the giants, but have these political reservations. I see it as a way of getting their own work popularised, but they haven't yet been able to effect social change either, because literature doesn't make much happen. They've been able to raise social awareness, but in terms of actual change not much has happened. Ben Okri is a second-generation writer but he's not in the tradition of socialist realism, because he doesn't reflect politics much in his writing. He lives in London, so he's far from his home base and does his own thing. The group I mentioned are all writing in Nigeria. Odia Ofeimun is a poet; Femi Osofisan is a dramatist; Kole Omotoso writes fiction; and Sowande writes fiction and drama. The whole thing may have died down now. They made a lot of noise in the late seventies and early eighties. It was a phase. They have critics like Biodun Jeyifo, who works in the same tradition, sponsoring them.

AC: African fiction seems to me to have a great strength in its depiction of the relationship between supernatural forces and the natural world, and also between the individual and public ritual; both are tensions that have been lost in much of European and American fiction. Do you agree? Is this changing?

OM: That's a good summary of what I've been trying to say. What is African realism? Realism in Africa embraces the supernatural and the natural. It doesn't distinguish. Myth and ritual are still very important in the life of the African and will remain so for a long time. It is part of an African worldview. This is a very interesting dimension to African realism, and the novel has to reflect this form of realism. There is a world we know, and a world we don't know. This impinges on ourselves, and on the writers. These worlds also interpenetrate, and influence each other on an everyday basis in Africa. The novel reflects this situation in Africa.

AC: Can African literature promote the meaning of citizenship and meaningful democracy when the state has so often been commandeered by military dictatorships? One almost needs to separate democracy as a voting system from a broader democracy. This affects how one discusses postcolonialism in Africa, because literature has a different role when people have the vote, and when there's a greater spread of education. Democracy almost becomes a technical thing in Africa, separate from the literature and culture in relation to the people.

OM: African literature can promote citizenship among those who read it. But a lot do not read it. Only the elites and students, but these are the future leaders of the nation. So this sense of citizenship may benefit them in the future. It's good for them to be aware of their responsibilities as citizens – so in that sense, yes. But we're returning to your first question about democracy, where I said that as long as there's poverty and mass ignorance, there will be a problem with democracy in Africa. Those who are rich and powerful will always have their way, and the army is always around to intervene. Perhaps in the far future when there's more intellectual enlightenment and a social welfare environment... but the political elite are very powerful and will have their way for a long time in Africa.

AC: Simon Gikandi writes that African literature "wills new African realities into being". Are there any forms of address now to a postcolonial future? How do you see the functions of storytelling in Africa developing in future?

OM: I have to tell you about developments in African fiction over the last ten years, the era of marvellous realism. Amos Tutuola's work evoked demons and supernatural powers; now there's been something of a return to Tutuola's tradition. Ben Okri is very influenced by Tutuola in *The Famished Road*. And in *Comes the Voyager at Last* Kofi Awoonor evokes past and present, natural and supernatural, turning to history, to the slave past and to the supernatural and mingling this with the present. That is part of what you may call marvellous realism. Syl Cheney-Coker of Sierra Leone, in *The Last Harmattan of Alusine Dunbar*, provides instances of marvellous realism.

So there has been some return to the evocation of the supernatural world. In the history of West African fiction, you have to take account of this development, but I believe it will fizzle out after a while. You will find writers returning to realistic fiction; the interface between fiction, politics, and history will continue. They have experimented with marvellous realism but this may not endure for long, because it is difficult to write in this form, and it is not very convincing. Eventually I believe writers will be discussing social reality, political corruption and the abuse of power. This will remain for a very long time the theme of African fiction, as long as corruption and misrule continue. I think that's the future of the African novel. There may be experimental diversions, but the dialogue between history, politics and the novel will continue for a long time.

Olive Schreiner: Life into Fiction

The main arguments against bioliterary criticism have been well formulated by B.A. Wright: "Arguing from the woman to the writer, seeking to interpret the writing by the medium of biography... assumes that the writer in action is identical with the woman engaged in her other activities... It assumes that what happens in the normal everyday world can explain what happens in a novel; that if an incident in a novel corresponds to an incident in the writer's life... we are thereby enabled to understand and interpret the novel... Conversely this kind of critic assumes that what happens in the novel can be brought in as biographical evidence, can enlighten us on what happened in real life. The distinction between the actual and the imaginary having been thus obliterated, it follows that circular arguments from biography to literature and back, in which fact and fiction vouch for each other, can be indulged in without restraint."[1] This distressing process is only too clearly in evidence in Schreiner's first biographers. S.C. Cronwright-Schreiner is very pleased to point out that he has found an actual Boer dance which was the original of the Boer wedding party in his wife Olive Schreiner's *The Story of an African Farm*, that old Otto is Schreiner's father, and that even Bonaparte Blenkins had an original, an Irishman living in Dordrecht.[2] Later his insistence on autobiographical elements in her fiction became reductive and resentful: "The Child's Day", the Prelude section to her novel *From Man to Man*, one of the finest interweavings of memory and imagination, with all kinds of thematic preparation for the story to follow, he calls "almost wholly autobiographical,"[3] thus perpetuating after her death a view of the Prelude she had deliberately countered during her life.[4]

Other early biographers were even more culpable in this area. Vera Buchanan-Gould, in her biography *Not Without Honour*, quotes directly or paraphrases badly from the fiction to describe events and processes in the life.[5] Schreiner is wholly identified with her heroines and the biographer shares with passionate indignation in what she sees as the noble, sublime, martyred lives of both. More than that, she is led by the imaginative intensity of certain scenes in the fiction to suggest or invent real-life parallels. The death of Albert Blair in the Diamond Fields in *Undine*, leads her to muse fondly: "was it possible that Julius Zaar (himself a fictitious person resulting from Gould's inability to read Schreiner's handwriting) had found his way to the Diamond Fields and died there?; or had Olive become interested in some other young man who had passed away in Kimberley?"[6] At other points Gould seems to feel the dangers of ignoring the imagination of someone whose genius she has constantly underlined, and whom she has compared with Socrates, Shelley, Emily Brontë, the tragic heroes of Aeschylus, and Jesus Christ, so she does offer the "salutary" reminder that Hardy "did not have to be a mother in order to understand the feelings of a girl who has an illegitimate baby."[7]

Circular bioliterary arguments from the life to the fiction arid back again mar the view of the person and the work in these early biographies. So do watered-down nineteenth-century stereotypes, such as that of an inexplicable "genius", whether it manifests itself as "the divine child"[8] seen by Havelock Ellis and S.C. Cronwright (at certain pressure points the "divine child" mutates into an "uncompromising baby"),[9] or the sublime female embodiment of the highest moral code and the noblest self-sacrifice (another Victorian stereotype, the "angel in the house"). This second creature, who lives in the adulation of female biographers and friends such as Vera Buchanan Gould, Ruth Alexander,[10] and Mary Brown,[11] is simply morally more perfect than anyone else, an angel on the koppie martyred by the coarse understandings of more limited beings, by the cruelty of her husband, and the scheming ploys of other women. (Gould sniffs at the machinations of Edith Lees who, she suggests, "stole" Ellis from Schreiner).[12] Anyone confronting Schreiner's life catches the whiff of gunpowder from ancient volleys fired in a battle of the sexes.

It's difficult not to join in.[13] Schreiner herself was often passionately partisan in relation to parents and husband, dropping hints about cruelty and neglect to favoured friends, blaming her lifelong asthma on her family's unkindness, separating from her husband with her lips sealed about the marriage (but sealed lips can be communicative). Most of the biographers take sides in the story of the Cronwright-Schreiner marriage. Gould simply assumes that all men are vicious seducers. Cronwright is definitely on his own side. Meintjes tells a story about a youthful seduction by Julius Gau (the mysterious "Zaar" above) without providing any sources.[14] First and Scott, supposedly sympathetic to their subject, very oddly accept completely Cronwright's view that his wife's accusations about other women must have been self-destructive delusions, paranoid and baseless (317).[15] This is where a lack of local material and South African contact has impeded biographers working from an intellectual base outside the country.[16]

This last point raises another problematic area in biographical work on Schreiner: the fact that she belonged to two cultures, and, for different periods of her life, lived in two different countries. Nor were these two countries "equivalent" in status, but were related in complicated ways through Imperial expansion, the question of power between metropolitan centre and colony which would be sharply raised by the activities of Cecil Rhodes in Africa and the Anglo-Boer war (both issues which would affect Schreiner intimately as person and writer), and the issue of cultural and intellectual differences between a European city and an African farm or village. The colonial predicament (rootedness without development or intellectual stimulus without emotional security), which held Schreiner hostage throughout her life, and of which *The Story of an African Farm* is one of the finest artistic expressions, becomes an intellectual watershed in the Schreiner biographies. Her biographers are either parochial in their patriotism, preferring Afrikaner culture to "the sick civilization of Europe" (Gould 133) and growing rhapsodic about the Karoo in a pastiche of Schreiner's own precisely realised epiphanies of African landscapes;[17] or they are expressions of British Jingoism (D.L. Hobman is as lyrical about Rhodes's English childhood as all the veld and vlei mystics of De Aar and Cradock are about mimosa bushes and red sand), or they are working from a metropolitan intellectual base which is far removed from the "grey pigments" of colonial life which surrounded

Schreiner's childhood, and into which she "sadly" but courageously dipped her pen.[18]

The First and Scott biography, the only one which has assimilated almost all the documentary evidence available on Schreiner, and which has openly and honestly tried to provide a modern synthesized view of the woman, acknowledging their sources at all points and striving for a scrupulous balance in their assessment, is nevertheless limited by its adherence to a later, and often rather rigid ideology shaped by Marx, Freud, and modern feminism. Instead of considering Schreiner's thought in relation to her writing, and her writings in relation to one another, they measure her "ideas" by the standards of the greatest and most influential minds in political theory and psychology, and by later theorists of the feminist movement. Not surprisingly, by these standards, they find Schreiner's "position" in these intellectual areas lacking. Furthermore, because Marxism is a materialist doctrine, they are suspicious of anything with overtones of the spiritual: missionary sentiment must be "pietistic";[19] literature is always a bit suspect, and it gets amazingly short shrift, especially when it veers toward "fantasy" and "dream";[20] and even the word "love" needs to be put in inverted commas, in case we think the biographers might believe in it.[21] Similarly, their dislike of the South African cause during the Boer War (because it was really only a struggle between two sets of rapacious white men ignoring the black population)[22] leads them to dismiss one of Schreiner's finest short stories, "Eighteen-ninety-nine", as "a rather maudlin account of the sufferings of women in wartime."[23] Here, a new brand of Marxist Jingoism and a failure of literary response triumph over the ostensible feminism of the biographers. At other junctures, their feminism rules their interpretations of crucial events, and of the fiction. *The Story of an African Farm*, the only novel they discuss at length apart from the juvenile work *Undine* (nevertheless a novel deserving more than the cursory and confused attention they give it), is discussed only in terms of its feminism, and almost completely in terms of Lyndall, ignoring the double protagonist situation which is central to the novel's structure and meaning. *Trooper Peter Halket of Mashonaland* is scarcely mentioned, and is omitted in the account of her oeuvre.[24] All of these priorities and emphases stem from S.C. Cronwright, whose assessment of Schreiner's life they intend to challenge. (Cronwright misspells "Halket" as "Halkett" throughout his biography, an amazing feat for one dedicated to proving that Schreiner could not spell!)

The First-Scott biography, in overturning the vague Romantic assumptions of inexplicable artistic "genius" unrooted in specific historical conditions, subjects Schreiner to a new imprisonment inside deterministic ideologies. Both Freudian psychology and the Marxist view of history are dedicated to the unmasking of the "latent" and thus more "real" determinants of a life in the repressed sexual conflicts of early experience and the socio-economic determinants of her historical period. Schreiner's asthma is thus linked to repressed sexual guilt; missionizing can be explained away as "a substitute for a sense of identity,"[25] and sometimes Marx and Freud are both used to relate the life causally to the fiction: "The European frontier society insulated itself from the indigenous society but internalised the violence it used against it;" hence the violence of Bonaparte and Tant Sannie's behaviour... .[26] The hindsight of modern feminism is sometimes used in an equally complacent way: they speak of "her own failed attempts to assert her needs and her autonomy as a woman."[27] Modern feminism often speaks from a position of enlightened strength which is more rhetorical than real.

Schreiner biography reveals a huge jump from the naive "life of a genius" approach to a knowing assessment of a Victorian neurotic. This is clearest in the different treatments of Schreiner's asthma, a crux for the Schreiner biographer. Gould and Hobman simply accept Schreiner's recurrent story that she was travelling in a coach and "got wet" (quite a relief, this explanation, in retrospect). Cronwright is characteristically concerned to impeach Schreiner's factual accuracy as to the date of the coach trip, the companions she had with her, and the towns between which she was travelling. First and Scott use a Freudian model of repressed sexual conflict: "was this because her awareness of her sexuality and its passion appalled her."[28] (211). Well, who knows?[29]

This cursory view of the extant Schreiner biographies[30] indicates problematic areas in the handling of a colonial woman writer's life, and in basic biographical methodology. The difficulties seem to be related partly to unquestioned assumptions about the relationship between an artist and society, and to unquestioned assumptions about the relationship between life and literature, or autobiography and fiction. "Life" is simply transcribed or imitated in fiction, though the "value" attached to the autobiographical element differs from biographer to biographer, Cronwright using the term reductively, Gould seeing it as an index to intensity and wisdom. There are problems of emotional distance (Cronwright's resentments about his fruitlessly sacrificed farm and his wife's failure to produce sufficient masterpieces to support them; the female Schwärmerei of Gould, Alexander, and Brown) and of geographical distance (writing from a sometimes patronizing metropolitan centre or from an uncritically perceived colonial culture). The latter problem is endemic to colonial, i.e. bi-partisan biography. In modern biography, the determinism inherent in recent ideologies, and underlying such a biography as that of First-Scott, has worked against the leverage given by a more thorough scrutiny of primary sources and a greater readiness to examine assumptions.

Some of the problems of Schreiner biography have fallen away as more material has become public or accessible. More clarity has been gained about her relationship with Karl Pearson in London, and this has been put to imaginative and illuminating use.[31] But given that "the biographer's material... is indeterminate and immeasurable; we can never be sure that we have it all, or all that is pertinent,"[32] the deeper problematic of an asthmatic feminist colonial woman writer's biography (one who wrote novels, political pamphlets, a polemical work on women, allegories, and a study of South Africa) – this problematic remains, and the time has come to suggest ways in which more justice can be done to the complex and dynamic interrelationship which exists between a writer's society, life and work, to the ways in which a writer can effect change as well as be affected by it, to the life and the work as a dialectical process instead of a static mimesis, to the very self of the writer as something endlessly being re-defined in memory, dream, prophecy and the symbolic self-projections of fiction. For a writer whose "dream life and real life"[33] were so intimately interwoven – perhaps for any writer – a more dynamic model is needed of the interaction between life and writing than that provided by deterministic ideologies, a model more in keeping with our own view of our lives as both determined and yet endlessly chosen, in which self-knowledge is always difficult and partial, and in which we are aware of both continuity and change.

In the biography of a writer the writing, both as act and product, should be central.[34] Literature should be both the instrument in and the aim of the clarification of the life. Both fantasy and autobiography need to be brought into relationship with the fiction, free of any *a priori* moral or historical disapproval. The writings need to be seen in relation to one another as well as in relation to their moment of composition, and the broader historical and social period to which they belong.[35]

As a first step, the "self of the writer should not be explained away by infantile fixations. Jung's rejection of Freud's "one-eyed" hypothesis is a pointer here: "Freud's mistake... was to reduce every present psychic condition to causes in the individual's past, never acknowledging that all psychic process constitutes a teleological chain as well as a causal one... psyche has not only come from somewhere; it is also going somewhere."[36] The self has also to be seen as less fixed and static: "The self is a fiction,"[37] endlessly in process, transforming itself into images; there is a never-ending "dialogue of a life with itself in search of its own absolute."[38] This process is everywhere in evidence in Schreiner's letters, her journals, her "Remembrances" about her ancestors and immediate family, her confidences to Havelock Ellis, and in her fiction. The oscillation between a stronger and weaker, regressive self is strikingly evident in her daily registration of mood in the constant letters which form an almost daily, intimate journal, even when no "official" journal was being kept.[39] Similarly, her fiction can illuminatingly be read as a symbolic conflict between opposing selves: her life is transformed into narrative both in her avowedly autobiographical writing and in her fiction: "every great work of fiction is simply an interior life in novel form". Every novel is "an autobiography by intermediary."[40] If one regards her fiction as a further extension, through the art of narrative, of the autobiographical impulse, then the "narrative offers us testimony of a woman about herself, the contest of a being in dialogue with itself, seeking its innermost fidelity."[41] (Gusdorf 43). This fruitful way of approaching fiction as autobiography is not reductive but creative, and it illuminates the life as well as the fiction; it has been formulated well by Gusdorf: "there is need of a second critique that instead of verifying the literal accuracy of the narrative or demonstrating its artistic value would attempt to draw out its innermost, private significance by viewing it as the symbol, as it were, or the parable of a consciousness in quest of its own truth."[42] (45).

The attempt that Schreiner made to transform herself into a "writer, a 'storyteller', was a lifelong one, from the moment she wrote to her elder sister affirming her new identity as "Olive Schreiner" and not the family baby, or the mother's help "Emily".[43] Her storytelling impulse, from a very early age, was a shaping impulse in which the amorphousness and difficulty of experience could be transmuted into narratives, whether they were oral compositions to invisible listeners, or the more self-consciously chosen genres of her later writing career. Story-telling established a reciprocity between self and world, teller and listener, past, present and future; "temporal perspectives thus seem to be telescoped together and to interpenetrate one another; they commune in that self-knowledge that regroups personal being above and beyond its own time limits."[44] This process is evident in Schreiner's "Remembrances" of her forebears as much as in her fiction. In her discussion of her ancestors she groups them into the opposed symbolic types, the dreamy German peasant and the dark cerebral woman, for instance, who reappear in her fiction. In the fiction her storytelling often offers contrasted or opposed biographies which enact the potentialities latent within her family and personal history, whether or not these "metaphors of self" are male or female, as in *The Story of an African Farm*, or both female, as in *From Man to Man*. They are opposed in terms of strength or weakness, oppressor or oppressed, and can take more explicitly colonial forms, as in *Trooper Peter Halket*, in the trooper and the black "victim" who exchange roles. Thus story-telling sets up a symbolic conflict of opposed selves, using a spectrum of names taken from family history ("Lyndall" and "Rebekah", her mother's names), from individual names ("Olive Emilie Albertina" was named after three dead brothers: "Em" the domestic and more passive woman appears in *African Farm*; interestingly, there is a male exploiter "Albert" Blair in *Undine* and an exploited "Bertie" in *From Man to Man*), and from the spiritual mentor Ralph Waldo Emerson ("Waldo" is thus a projected "transcendental" self and Emersonian dreamer in *African Farm*).

These symbolic self-projections involve memory as well as fantasy, recollection as well as prophecy. Jane Austen coined the phrase "artificial memory"[45] which seems to describe the blend of artifice and recollection which goes into the shaping of the lives of invented characters in a novel. There are strikingly similar processes at work in Schreiner's autobiographical writing and her fiction: memory, fantasy,[46] anecdote, dream and prophecy make up strong elements in both kinds of writing, with different degrees of conscious shaping: "The passage from immediate experience to consciousness in memory, which effects a sort of repetition of that experience, also serves to modify its significance... it has won a new and more intimate relationship to the individual life that can thus... be rediscovered and drawn together again beyond time."[47] This comment recognizes that recollected experience is different when it is used inside a fictional narrative; it is part of a new order reconstituted beyond ordinary time. Certain key "memories" are used by Schreiner in this way: a childhood sacrifice scene in *Undine* and in *African Farm*, each in a different narrative context; the building of a stone house for mice in *From Man to Man*, the beating of a child or animal in those three novels; a child telling stories to others in *African Farm* and *From Man to Man*. In all of her novels there are childhood scenes either as prelude or backdrop to the main action: reconstituted memories are a method of positing the continuity of the self through time. The epigraph to *African Farm* reads: "The entire man is, so to speak, to be found in the cradle of the child." The titles of the two sections of From Man to Man posit the same continuity: "The Child's Day" and "The Woman's Day"; the shift to female pronouns is a key shift in emphasis to the problems of continuity in female identity with which the later novel is concerned.

If Schreiner's life can be seen as that of a "broken and untried possibility"[48] – and her biographers have generally tried to account for what they read as failure, either connected with a genius born before its time, or with grievously unresolved conflicts, or with the failure to write or complete more fictional work – then it might be true to say that "every life, even in spite of the most brilliant successes, knows itself inwardly botched"[49] and that the writing of autobiography or fiction constitutes an avowal of wholeness through a designed self-confrontation: "To create and in creating be created."[50]

Although Schreiner's fiction rests on a symbolic conflict of opposed selves locked into frustration and conflict, it also moves toward moments of "vision" or epiphanies which illuminate these conflicts. Such epiphanies are associated with nature or with death, sometimes both (as in Waldo's death scene in *African Farm*). In the moment of natural death, Schreiner offers the epiphany from beyond time to set over against the world of process which is also the world of decay.

> The image that we hold or are given at such moments is a vision of human life raised to a symbolic, a more-than-human significance; or, if we turn it around, it is a picture of our own potential psychic wholeness... a figure of completeness which is the end of all psychic endeavour.[51]

If biography is a skill which seeks to bring the writer's life and work into illuminating relationship, then the new directions offered by the creative study of fiction as a form of autobiography seem to offer a more dynamic and flexible model of such interrelationships than has been hitherto available.

Notes

This paper was delivered at a conference of the European Association of Commonwealth Literature and Language Studies, Sitges, Spain, April 1984.

1. Wright 13-14. I have altered the wording to suit Schreiner's case.

2. Cronwright-Schreiner Life 115, 148.

3. Cronwright-Schreiner "Introduction" 17.

4. She was hurt by Cronwright's response to the Prelude when she sent it to him, and later sent it to Mrs Francis Smith (October 1909) explaining that it was "a picture in small, a kind of allegory, of the life of the woman in the book." She also described it as "the incarnation of my own childhood." The two comments suggest the impersonal, artistic use of memory. See Letters section in C. Clayton (ed.) *Olive Schreiner*, McGraw Hill, 1983, p.122, and p.126. First and Scott take over Cronwright's view of the Prelude, cf *Olive Schreiner*, Deutsch, 1980, footnote to p.182.

5. Gould 18, 23, 40, 48, for instance.

6. Ibid 50.

7. Ibid 72.

8. Cronwright-Schreiner Life 176.

9. Ibid 345.

10. Ruth Alexander was very angered by the image of Schreiner presented by S.C. Cronwright in his *Life and Letters*. She intended to publish a counter-attack in her own edition of Schreiner's letters, but this did not materialize. See her review of Cronwright's *Life*, *The South African Nation*, 9 August 1924: p. 21.

11. Mary Brown, "Recollections of Olive Schreiner" in *The Life of Mrs John Brown*, edited by Angela James and Nina Hills, John Murray, 1937, pp. 183-205.

12. Gould 119.

13. Accusations against Schreiner's mother are countered by K.E. Jones, "In defence of Rebecca Schreiner," *Forum*, vol. 4, no. 3, 1955, pp.38-40. Many of the memoirists and reviewers take sides in the story of the marriage. Recently Guy Butler has published S.C. Cronwright's 1921 diary of *The Re-interment on Buffelskop* to provide more insight into Cronwright's side of the story (Grahamstown: Institute for the study of English in Africa, Rhodes University, 1983).

14. Meintjes 21.

15. First 317

16. Though there is no evidence of actual sexual infidelity on Cronwright's side, there is evidence of lifelong intimate and flirtatious correspondence with a young girl, Ethel Friedlander, and with Mrs. I. Philpot, the woman Cronwright accused Schreiner of being insanely obsessed about. See the Friedlander/Cronwright corre-

spondence, private collection of Mrs. E. Horwitz, Johannesburg.

17. Hobman 115. Many occasional pieces have appeared linking Schreiner a little sentimentally with the Karoo landscape.

18. See Schreiner's Preface to the second edition of *The Story of an African Farm*, reprinted in most editions.

19. First 37.

20. Ibid 21, 182.

21. Ibid 16.

22. I make this point not because I do not sympathize with this view of the Anglo-Boer war, but because it is another instance of their ahistorical view of Schreiner to cite a view developed mainly after the war against someone whose loyalties crystallized out in the midst of the conflict, and who was clearsighted enough to see the role of British capitalism in precipitating the war.

23. First 247.

24. Ibid 12.

25. Ibid 45.

26. Ibid 97.

27. Ibid 16.

28. First 211.

29. Perhaps Havelock Ellis knew. At any rate, his case-history of Schreiner's sexual development, in *Studies in the Psychology* of Sex Vol. III (Philadelphia: F.A. Davis, 1928) Appendix B, History IX, does not indicate that she was any more appalled by her own sexuality than the average woman.

30. There have been other surveys of the extant biographies. One of the more recent is Patricia Morris's "Biographical Accounts of Olive Schreiner", in *Olive Schreiner and After*, edited by M. van Wyk Smith & Don Maclennan, David Philip, 1983. She concludes that "The definitive biography exists only in each reader's reading." I do not agree that we need be that pessimistic about the necessary subjectivity of biography. Schreiner's own view of the limitations of biography is worth quoting. After commending Lewes's life of Goethe (she was herself an avid reader of biographies) she comments:

> A man can only write the life of a man whom he understands, and of whom he understands not only one side but all the important sides, and Lewes was particularly fitted to understand Goethe. Most people seem to think any smart writer who gets all the documents about him can write of any man. The older one gets the more one realizes there can be no absolutely true life of anyone except written by themselves, and then only if written for the eye of God. Only after long years looking back does one really understand oneself sometimes. Letter to

Ellis, 6 November 1907, in *The Letters of Olive Schreiner*, edited by S.C. Cronwright-Schreiner, Unwin, 1924, p. 274.

31. See Betty McGinnis Fradkin, "Olive Schreiner and Karl Pearson" *Quarterly Bulletin of the South African Library*, vol. 3, no. 4, 1977, pp.84-93, Fradkin's discussion of Pearson is related to Schreiner's literary development, unlike First-Scott's.

32. Wright 15.

33. The title of a Schreiner short story, and of the 1893 volume of short works which took its name from the story.

34. The corollary is that a biographer of a literary figure should also be a literary critic. F.R. Karl's recent biography of Joseph Conrad (*Three Lives*, Faber & Faber, 1979) seems to fulfil both functions.

35. James Olney, in his "Autobiography and the Cultural Moment" (in *Autobiography* edited by Olney, Princeton University Press, 1980), refers to Erik H. Erikson's work in "Gandhi's Autobiography: The Leader as Child" in *Life History and the Historical Moment*: "he shows how as students of autobiography we should fix autobiographical events in the moment of writing and in the history of the writer and his time... it is memory that reaches tentacles out into each of these three different "times" – the time now, the time then, and the time of an individual's historical context." In the second section of this paper, I have drawn heavily on Olney's work, on that of the contributors to his edition of essays in *Autobiography*, and on Olney's *Metaphors of Self: The Meaning of Autobiography* (Princeton University Press, 1972). I have not been able to deal with the issue of historical context in this paper, but I think the evangelism and missionary imperialism of Schreiner's period have literary potentialities which have not yet been explored (such as character oppositions between saint and rogue, patterns of dissent, the didactic use of deathbed scenes, etc.). For a study of Schreiner's novels in the context of late 19th and early 20th century cultural history see Preben Kaarsholm's "Lutheranism and Imperialism in the Novels of Olive Schreiner" (in *Kultur og Samfund* Institut VI, Roskilde Universitetscenter, 1983).

36. Olney *Metaphors* 117-118).

37. Olney *Autobiography* 22. Olney discusses the three terms of autobiography (autos-self; bios- self; "graphy"-the writing) and argues that it is through the act of writing "that the self and the life, complexly intertwined and entangled, take on a certain form, assume a particular shape and image, and endlessly reflect that image back and forth between themselves as between two mirrors" (22). See also J. Hillis Miller, *The Form of Victorian Fiction* (University of Notre Dame, 1970) for a discussion of these endlessly reflected selves in the narrative structure of Victorian fiction, what he calls the "Quaker Oats box effect."

38. Gusdorf 48.

39. There is a fine description of a self being broken and re-made in Bessie Head's description of the female protagonist, also an artist, in *Maru* (Heinemann, 1971):

"You were never sure whether she was greater than you, or inferior, because of this constant flux and inter-change between her two images... her breaking point could so clearly be seen – as though one part of her broke down and was mended by another, and so on" (7).

40. These two last quotations are from Gusdorf in Olney, p.46. They expand the definition of the novel offered by G. Lukacs in his *Theory of the Novel* (Merlin Press, 1978) that "the outward form of the novel is essentially biographical" (77).

41. Gusdorf 43.

42. Ibid 45.

43. In a letter to Kate Schreiner, 11th April 1871, The Findlay Letters, Cullen Library, University of the Witwatersrand, Johannesburg.

44. Gusdorf 44.

45. To describe Fanny Price in *Mansfield Park* (Penguin, 1966, p.186).

46. Ellis mentions her development of sexual fantasy in his case-history.

47. Gusdorf 38.

48. Her phrase about herself used as a final chapter heading by First and Scott.

49. Gusdorf 39.

50. Ibid 44.

51. Jung quoted by Olney in *Metaphors of Self,* pp. 126-127.

"A World Elsewhere:"
Bessie Head as Historian

Bessie Head emigrated to Botswana in 1964, at the age of 26, two years before the territory became independent. Her departure was not for overtly political reasons, though she was given an exit permit only, and remained a stateless person until granted Botswana citizenship in 1979. She left because of the breakdown of her marriage, the economic lure of a teaching post in Botswana, and her despair at being unable to function as a "storyteller" in a country of rigidly enforced racial separation, which made both personal stability and a sense of human community difficult to achieve.[1] The leap into Botswana was not, as it has sometimes been for others,[2] to mount a writer's guerrilla attack against the South African state, but to anchor her writing life in a sustaining human context ("the warm embrace of the brotherhood of man")[3] which would free her from the tyranny of anger,[4] and from a concentration on the more superficial manifestations of the policy of apartheid in order to attack, from a broader Africanist base, the distortion of the South African system. Her project as a writer, both as novelist and historian (I want to suggest that these functions fuse in *A Bewitched Crossroad*, her last book) has been complex, relying on an interweaving of Western literacy and the African oral tradition, thus creating, in its artistic matrix, an imaginative equivalent of her moral and social ideal for Southern Africa. She saw herself, rightly, as a pioneer, parallel to an earlier white South African pioneer, Olive Schreiner, but distinguished from her by her wider African stance, her concern "with African questions as a whole."[5]

I wish to argue that Bessie Head's final historical "novel", *A Bewitched Crossroad* (1984), is the fullest statement of her critique of

South African history and society, because its reach into the Southern African past illuminates the complex causes of two contrasted colonial fates, and this comparative base enables her to project an ideal platform for a Southern African future:

> It would seem as though Africa rises at a point in history where world trends are more hopefully against exploitation, slavery and oppression all of which has been synonymous with the name, Africa. I have recorded whatever hopeful trend was presented to me in an attempt to shape the future, which I hope will be one of dignity and compassion.[6]

By embedding her act of protest within a celebration of a freer, more benevolent culture and society, one with a "flat continuity"[7] of basic existence, Head wins for herself and her project a degree of freedom from the constriction within the protest paradigm which has been the dominant mode for the black South African writer, a mode in itself determined by the structures of apartheid. This space for literary manoeuvre was engineered by her departure from the literal, imprisoning "space" of South Africa to a country where there was more human dignity, where she could think, and morally compare, where her own feeling for humour, individuality, unpredictability and story-telling could operate.[8] Delighted by the miracle of her arrival, after three novels and one collection of stories, in a relatively clear outer and inner space (this arrival is imaged only at the end of her third novel, *A Question of Power*, after the negative psychic poison of apartheid has been outered)[9] she turns to the history of the country which she has just claimed in a "gesture of belonging: "She placed one soft hand over her land."[10] The gesture is that of the woman writer claiming her writer's territory.

How was it, she then seems to ask, that this country was miraculously preserved from the colonial storm of hatred and destruction? She set out to "record, in a constructive way, the past history of the Bamangwato;[11] "to trace those roots of freedom."[12] The answers she finds are couched in the terms suggested to her by her own subjective response to the broken sense of history, and the humiliation she had known in South Africa. She writes of Ellen Kuzwayo's book, *Call Me Woman*, that "at the end of the book one feels as if a shadow history of South Africa had been written."[13] One could adapt this image and say that Head's historical work on Botswana subtends at every point the shadow of the South African nightmare. It has been argued of the historical imagination that "the gulf of time between the historian and his object must be bridged. The object must be of such a kind that it can revive itself in the historian's mind; the historian's mind must be such as to offer a home for that revival... his thought must be pre-adapted to become its host."[14] Bessie Head's "thought" is the perfect host for Botswana history, in that the qualities she finds in it are those she needs to heal the damaged areas in her sense of the South African past. Psychological need triggers intellectual curiosity and creates the imaginative arena of the mind on which Botswana's "unique colonial history"[15] could be recreated. Almost any comparative point illustrates this relationship. Where her South African past was broken and fragmented, Botswana society has the quality of "wovenness" and "wholeness";[16] where South African politics had a quality of nightmarish irrationality, Botswana politics was largely rational; where African leaders in South Africa had been ruthlessly suppressed, imprisoned, or driven underground, in Botswana African leaders of stature, diplomacy and power had emerged; where African traditions had been downgraded, ignored and crushed in South Africa in a brutally evolving Western capitalist economy, in Botswana African customs had been able to drop elements of darkness and cruelty associated with human sacrifice, and, under the Christian leadership of Chief Khama III, had flexibly accommodated the basic spirit of Christian teaching. Where black people in South Africa had been humiliated, ousted from their own land, deprived of citizenship, turned into a landless proletariat, and denied their human dignity, in Botswana, by a sequence of lucky accidents and good management, all of these evils had been avoided. It is this "miracle" of historical luck which becomes her subject in her historical "novel" *A Bewitched Crossroad* (1984).

The main danger of such a relationship between historian and subject would be that of idealization, and Head has acknowledged the danger.[17] She compares her own initial responses to the Batswana people with those of a Jewish artist, Josef Herman, who painted disproportionately large portraits of people in a Welsh village after escaping the Nazi invasion of Poland. She says "I found a similar peace in Botswana village life and also drew large and disproportionate portraits of ordinary people. I meant that the immense suffering black people experience in South Africa had created in me a reverence for ordinary people."[18] She worked through this attitude in her first historical book, *Serowe: Village of the Rain Wind* (1981), in which ordinary Serowe inhabitants tell their own story, and though there is authorial selection of oral history to illustrate her topics (self-help, social reform, the London Missionary Society, the beginnings of education, medical services) there is a minimum of authorial intervention in the actual narrative, which is composed of first-person statements by her interviewees.

Serowe; Village of the Rain Wind is the germ of the later book, *A Bewitched Crossroad*, and many of the elements and procedures of her "African saga" are present in Serowe in a different proportion and emphasis; they lie loosely in a less deeply fused structure. She suggests that the history of Serowe is "precariously oral,"[19] and implies that she is offering her literacy, her skills as a scribe, to the people who have taken her in as a South African refugee.[20] The book opens and closes with two key elements of her perception of Botswana, elements which become in *A Bewitched Crossroad* recurrent images of a continuity deeper than historical change: birdsong and the dreaming horizons:

> And why is it always one bird-call I hear at dawn? It is always one bird that starts the day for me, outside my window, and he's not saying anything very properly-just a kind of hesitant "peep-peep" as though he's half-scared at opening his eyes. But the light outside, at dawn, is unearthly too – a kind of white light; an immense splash of it along an endless horizon. This white light quickly pulsates into a ball of molten gold and here in the sunrise, you can time the speed of the earth's rotation as the enormous fiery ball arises. It is barely a minute before it breaks clear of the flat horizon. It scares me. I say to myself:

"What the hell am I doing on something that moves so fast?"[21]

Birdsong, horizons and the Botswana hills, blue and misty in the distance but up close "flat and unmysterious surfaces like the uncombed heads of old Batswana men,"[22] are associated in *A Bewitched Crossroad* with the old man Sebina, the oral memory of the tribe and the witness to its critical changes. Here it is Head herself who stands at this poised moment, hearing the timeless bird-call (is it the same bird or simply the same song), looking at the distant view and contemplating the cosmic scale but aware of the closer reality, the un-mysterious surface of hills without mist. Such moments become, in her historical novel, the crossroads at which the historian and the novelist intersect. The same elements recur in the epilogue to *Serowe* called "A Poem to Serowe," in which the author frames her oral testimony by her own response to the village, at once lyrical and practical, penetrated with the quality of thought, the subjective consciousness which holds together the collected data, portraits, testimony:

> The hours I spent collecting together my birds, my pathways, my sun-sets, and shared them, with everyone; The small boys of the village and their homemade wire cars; The windy nights, when the vast land mass outside my door simulates the vast roar of the ocean. And those mysteries: that one birdcall at dawn – that single solitary outdoor fire-place far in the bush that always captivates my eye. Who lives so far away in the middle of nowhere? The wedding parties and the beer parties of my next-door neighbours that startle with their vigour and rowdiness; The very old women of the village who know so well how to plough with a hoe; their friendly motherliness and insistent greet-ings as they pass my fence with loads of firewood or water buckets on their heads; My home at night and the hours I spent inside it with long solitary thought.
>
> These small joys were all I had, with nothing beyond them, they were indulged in over and over again, like my favourite books.[23]

Solitude and community, inside and outside views, the solitary thinker whose candlelit space corresponds with the "solitary outdoor fireplace" in the bush, the loud communal rites, the lonely writer who is yet "insistently" greeted by passersby, the intellectual who imag-inatively collects and shares like the women gathering firewood, the comparison of life with "favourite books," life as book-this is the imaginative site, the semi-assimilated position of the intellectual in exile, from which Bessie Head creates her historical world, the "Bo-tswana of my own making."[24] The exile here, unlike the despairing South African exile in an anonymous, urbanized European culture, is able to create an imaginative bridge between self and community, to find new correlatives (that solitary fireplace in the bush) for the self, to penetrate with thought, and thus re-create in fiction, the adopted environment. There is also something decisively female about this ne-gotiation of space, the emotional anchoring imaged here: the intellec-tual is a woman who needs to be sufficiently in touch with those older women and their "friendly motherliness" in order to collect and share with everyone "my birds, my pathways, my sunsets."[25]

A Bewitched Crossroad, which Head calls a "novel" and an "African saga," and which invokes "the spirit of Ulysses" in its opening pages,[26] grows out of the brief historical appendix to *Serowe*. Its key invention is the lightly fictionalized story of Sebina, a leader of a Bamangwato clan whose successful fusion with Khama's people transfers Head's own emigration to Botswana into a retrospective historical frame. One old man's lifespan becomes the focalizing thread drawn through the historical tapestry.[27] He stands for a core of tribal memory amidst change and upheaval, and for one confluence of African tradition and Western innovation (*Khama the Great*, 1875-1923, is another). His openness to the new is valourized in comparison with both "closed" tribalists and "closed" missionaries.[28] He represents a flexibility of spirit as against a rejected ideological rigidity. Head's narrative, which forestalls closure in its treatment of time, and its cyclical structure, embodies this spirit as formal protest.

A Bewitched Crossroad is a corrective historical study: it overturns Eurocentric colonial myths and advances an evenhanded and convincing re-reading of Southern African history. It draws both on Head's international intellectual reading and scholarship, and on her deep sympathy with the African past. A key emphasis which appears in *A Bewitched Crossroad* is the idea of great leaders, those who made great gestures and "great gestures have an oceanic effect on society – they flood a whole town."[29] The idea of benevolent leadership, of a chief who, like Khama the Great "carved out a new road for the tribe,"[30] is a shaping pressure in Head's earlier novel *Maru*. In *Serowe*, the history of the town is given in the three phases and portraits of Khama the Great, his son Tshekedi Khama, and the white South African Patrick van Rensburg, who contributed to the development of Botswana by initiating and developing the Swaneng Project for academic and technical training. Thus the portraits themselves reflect Head's emphasis on a multi-racial, assimilative leadership. Her emphasis on great leaders or chiefs has a double root: an African tradition of praise and worship for the austere, quietly effective chief of the tribe, and the reverence given by an ex-South African to leaders who are powerful without being oppressive, who use their power for

the benefit of the community at large. Once again, this runs counter to South Africa, where whiteheads of state have been leaders of
a powerful minority, and have exerted their power in divisive and
oppressive ways. In *A Bewitched Crossroad* the image of Khama the
Great becomes a bulwark against colonial invasion and the expropri-
ation of land. His diplomatic use of his Christian reputation in Britain
to fuse supportive philanthropic groups against Cecil Rhodes is contrasted with brutal power-mongers like Rhodes himself, and with an
older style of African chief such as Shaka of the Zulus, and especially
Mzilikazi of the Matabele. The Matabele (the name was derogatory of
the Ndebele, meaning "non-people") are seen as indiscriminate killers,
black parallels to the darkness in Rhodes's heart:

> It was as though an inhuman brute force, that was almost a kind
> of... dull illiteracy, informed the heart of the Ndebele nation. It was
> as though like were finally meeting like in the person of Cecil John
> Rhodes, for an inhuman brute force informed his heart too. All his
> utterances were ugly.[31]

Khama, in contrast, represents the literate heart. The acceptance
of Christianity by the Bamangwato went hand in hand with the acceptance of "schooling", making "the Book speak", and Head uses
character oppositions in *A Bewitched Crossroad* to illustrate reactionary attitudes toward the new learning as against the receptivity of the
eager, progressive section of the people.

The character in the novel who represents a fear of literacy and
education also represents a reactionary attitude toward the reforms
Khama introduced to equalize the situation of men and women. He
abolished "bogadi", or the bride price, which had tied a woman and
her children (even the children of her second marriage) in perpetuity
to one man's family. He thus gave women economic independence,
and an equivalent right to divorce. Maruapula, the man who prevents
his son from attending the missionary school, is enraged by these
measures to free women, and clings to the wisdom of the tribe, en-
shrined in the proverb "A woman is a little dog (to be fondled and
kicked)."[32] Again, progress is imagined as "dialogue between a man
and a woman."[33] Head's terms echo other definitions of sexual equality: where no speech is repressed on either side, where women have
an equal right to make their voices heard, as Khama allows women to

plead their own cases in the chiefs's "kgotla" (place for the settlement of disputes). Fullness of speech is also what she confers on her "characters," both real (in *Serowe*) and fictional. Head's attitude is complex, here, as elsewhere: she allows another image of woman to rest side by side with the new image of sexual dialogue:

> Slowly the old man walked through the village.... He paused a while near a yard where a tall, slender woman pounded corn in a stamping block with a long wooden pestle, her bare feet partly buried in a growth of summer grass.
>
> It was a scene that had been before him all his life but it seemed as fresh and new as creation itself. Her form swayed to and fro with the rhythm of her work, her face closed and withdrawn in concentration.
>
> The warm slanting rays of the late afternoon sunlight seemed to transfix that timeless moment in his memory like every other moment of happiness for him.[34]

This timeless moment, like the moment of birdsong a point of stasis around which the historical narrative is slung, rests on a familiar vision of woman as silent icon."[35] Enmeshed in tradition, she becomes representative of it. Head allows this moment to co-exist with the liberating moment in Chapter 12; such moments co-exist in Southern African reality. Her narrative is hospitable to such opposed modes of perception; in this respect it embodies in its unjudging tolerance a quality she is celebrating in Chief Khama, and in Bamangwato society as a whole.

A Bewitched Crossroad is also culturally and linguistically hospitable. The happy co-existence of modern idiom and African proverb, the constant drawing on traditional song and legend, the use of the San tradition of laughter as defence and as one of the hiding-places of the spirit,[36] the structuring of the novel around one old man's memory as the repository of the tribe's history and yet a modern researcher's use of documentary archives-style and structure cohere tightly with moral statement and social ideal. Historical documents are skilfully deployed to reveal the greed and corruption of Rhodes, and the pathos of the African chiefs' appeals to Britain for help when threatened by Boer invasion:

> Such a prospect is not one to which we can look forward except with weeping and distress and we beg of you to help us if there can be

found a means of escape and we will thank you with all our hearts. We refuse thus to be cast away.[37]

At other junctures (and much of the historical material is mediated by tribal discussion, and response) historical crisis is summed up by an African speaker in his own idiom, such as Lobengula's remark as he realizes that Britain's granting of the Charter to Rhodes for the exploration of Matabeleland and Mashonaland heralded the devastation of his kingdom:

> Did you ever see a chameleon catch a fly? The chameleon gets behind the fly and remains motionless for sometime then he advances very slowly and gently, first putting forward one leg and then another. At last, when well within reach he darts his tongue and the fly disappears. England is the chameleon and I am that fly.[38]

Humour, with its connotations of personal resilience and tolerance, plays a key role in Head's vision of African leadership. Moshoeshoe, chief of the Basotho, decisively veers away from killing and confrontation when the leader of the cannibals who had eaten his grandfather is brought to him for trial. Moshoeshoe responds to demands for vengeance by saying that he does not wish to disturb the grave of his ancestor. Humour precedes compassion: "Men cannot eat stones," he adds, "let it all be forgotten."[39] This incident is seen as a decisive moment for African history because it breaks with the tradition of the Mfecane, the tribal "Wars of Calamity" (approximately 1817-1837) which had led to starving hordes of people sweeping across the interior of Southern Africa. Humour implies a yielding, a softening of stance, and Head sees such moments as critical in the humanizing of a military society, the dismantling of a war machine.

Moshoeshoe is seen as a forerunner of Khama the Great (Lesotho, the landlocked territory within South Africa, is the remnant of Moshoeshoe's kingdom and a smaller independent parallel to Botswana in modern South Africa). The spatial memory of the narrative is organized around such precedents and recurrences.[40] For instance, Khama's proclamation at the granting of the Protectorate is first given in brief quotes, extracts, hints and guesses; finally it is given in full. It demonstrates an African chief's ability to command literacy as a safeguard in the negotiation of terms with a European power. The document also fixes, in the new form of documentary preservation, the "cultural dialogue"[41] of the tribe's past which had been perfected in Khama, so its emergence within the narrative is in itself a key moment where the oral past meets a Western cultural habit. The narrative rests on a tension between oral memory, including in Sebina "its own image of the memory's functioning,"[42] and documentation, or textuality. The history of Southern Africa is a tale of exploited illiteracy, dishonest missionary witnesses, and crooked documents. Lobengula's kingdom was stolen from him by such ruses. Head's endorsement of literacy is thus not merely socially progressive; it is a form of artistic protection running counter to the morally offensive strategies of the European exploitation of Africa.

Although *A Bewitched Crossroad* is a historical "novel", it constitutes a decisive modern historical judgment of colonial history, presented from an African point of view. It shows how Khama's Christian image in Britain, the fortunate intervention of the British to "protect" Bechuanaland (though for motives corrupted by self-interest)[43] and Rhodes's overreaching action in planning the Jameson Raid, together led to the miraculous escape of Bechuanaland from the hand of the Chartered Company. Bechuanaland lay in a geographical bottleneck and is arid country: its defects helped to save it. The Jameson Raid was also a historical bottleneck, or, as in Olive Schreiner's view, the crucial event which, in initiating a more rapacious phase of imperialism in Southern Africa and the second Anglo-Boer War, would permanently drive the Afrikaner back into a hostile and self-justifying republicanism, and give him his historical charter to oppress the indigenous population.[44] Bessie Head is presenting the other side of this coin: the Jameson Raid triggered the tragic fate of South Africa but preserved Bechuanaland for African pastoralists. South Africa became a place where Africans could not dream; where magic was banished for tortures both bureaucratic and real.[45] Botswana became the bewitched crossroad.

By showing that Southern Africa was never Livingstone's "dark continent"[46] for the African people, or the tabula rasa of colonial mythology where "dreamers" like Rhodes could inscribe their fantasies,[47] but a real site where cultures met, conflicted, gave way or peaceably meshed, Head overturns a dominant colonial myth. By showing the African people as moral agents within their own landscape, revealing "a people with a delicate nervous balance like everyone else,"[48] she activates believable and varied human beings whose inner life is acted upon by credible historical events, and who seek, in turn, to encounter and shape history."[49] Sebina's tale – of a life dried up in despair by the oppression of the Matabele, but joyfully re-activated by his decision to lead his clan to Khama's territory-is precisely such a story. Head's strong sense of historical causation, as in her handling of the relationship between the Mfecane and the Great Trek ("It could be said that from 1836 onwards, the Dutch Trekboer moved into the vacuum of the depopulated central highveld, depopulated by the Mfecane Wars," p. 27), decentres the Great Trek from its position as overriding historical and literary myth.[50] The Trek becomes only one, and not the most significant, of a pattern of continental tribal migrations. In *A Bewitched Crossroad* the old man, Sebina, witnesses many tribal migrations, the fourth of which takes him from Shoshong to the new capital of Palapye. Head instals him in his wagon in a striking new image of the African trekker:

> The old man placed one timeworn hand on the wooden rail of the open wagon to steady himself. Above the bouncing roll of the wagon and the sound of steadily marching feet in the lull of song from the children, came the call of birdsong.[51]

Sebina, then, in his role as historical witness to every era of Southern African change, with one hand on the wagon's rail and his vision fixed "on the flat open plains and dreaming hills,"[52] in his loyalty to tradition and his openness to novelty, is an internal narrative image for Bessie Head as author and historical witness. Testifying with accuracy to an African historical past, with its emergent Christian humanism, becomes a judgment on a country where Christianity seems to have been able to exclude humanism. Head stresses the wording of the Great Trek manifesto which distinguished between an "elect" and mere "Schepsels," i.e. creatures or slaves.[53] Christianity as Calvinist predestination applied to fixed racial categories has served as the foundation and rationalization of apartheid. Head's critique of South Africa thus bypasses the details of apartheid to attack its base. She witnesses to an absence by celebrating an African presence in the history of Botswana. In doing so, she fulfils another function of the historian: "Die Weltgeschichte ist das Weltgericht".[54] She modifies this dictum by making her history of one country a moral, human judg-ment on another. Her unique position as a black woman historian in Southern Africa leads her to overturn a dominant settler mythology and to correct the harshness of the frontier spirit in favour of what she calls, in *The Collector of Treasures*, a "compromise of tenderness"[55] between African tradition and Western influence. Her own deeply tested benevolence validates her enterprise. And through her recent death she recedes into the history of the country she chronicled:

> Historical thought is of something which can never be a this, because it is never a here and now. Its objects are events which have finished happening.... Only when they are no longer perceptible do they be-come objects for historical thought.[56]

As I turn and regard her, from the current crossroad of South African history, her death liberates her writer's image, and the whole-ness of her oeuvre, from the broken and stressed realities of her ac-tual life. Her writer's image becomes healed, freed from accident and change, suprareal. By making this move, I see that she, too, is a sub-jective construct, a "Bessie Head of my own making," an image of wholeness and benevolence urgently needed at the current moment. A double historicity, of object and beholder, stands revealed.

Notes

1. See "Let Me Tell a Story Now...," *The New African*, September 1962, and "Letter from South Africa," *Transition* vol. 3, no. 11, 1963, which express her sense of frustration in South Africa. She tells of her departure from South Africa in a fairly extensive interview with Jean Marquard, ("Bessie Head: Exile and Community in Southern Africa," *London Magazine*, vol. 18, no. 9 & 10, 1978-1979: pp.48-61.)

2. Black poet Mongane Wally Serote also left South Africa for Botswana, and his novel, *To Every Birth Its Blood* (Ravan, 1981), is a useful point of comparison because it traces the conversion of a young man to "the movement" of revolutionary activity: it is more explicitly aimed at political consciousness-raising, and ends in a metaphor of a young woman giving "birth" to a new African order. When Head writes a preface to a South African historical work like Sol. T. Plaatje's *Native Life in South Africa* (Ravan, 1982), she speaks of the book's "appeal to a day of retribution" (xiii). Her own aims seem more in keeping with another comment she makes on Plaatje: "Plaatje acknowledges that black people have no power so his main aim is to present the black personality as deserving justice, humanity and dignity" (Preface xi).

3. Head *Question* 206

4. Ezekiel Mphahlele, in *The African Image*, discusses the issue of anger for the black South African writer: "the artistic difficulty that arises when one is angry most of the time and when one's sense of values is continually being challenged by the ruling class" (Faber, 1962, p. 53).

5. Marquard "Bessie" 52-53.

6. Head "Notes" 32.

7. Head *Serowe* xi.

8. "South Africa is a land where history proceeds up to the present day in events of unrelieved horror, untouched by human tenderness, charm and unpredictability." Foreword to *Native Life in South Africa*, p. xii.

9. There is an excellent discussion of the societal framework, and societal causes, of Elizabeth's breakdown in *A Question of Power* by Adetokunbo Pearse in "Apartheid and Madness: Bessie Head's *A Question of Power*," *Kunapipi*, vol. 5, no. 2, 1983, pp.81-93.

10. Head *Question* 206.

11. The tribal name, Bamangwato, "reaches out and embraces all the refugees and diverse nations absorbed into the small Bangwato clan during the era of nation building by chiefs Sekigoma I and Khama III" (Author's Note, *A Bewitched Crossroad*, Ad. Donker, 1984).

12. Marquard "Bessie" 50, 51.

13. Foreword to Ellen Kuzwayo's *Call Me Woman*, Ravan, 1985, p. xiv.

14. Collingwood 304.

15. Head "Writing" 21.

16. Head *Serowe* x.

17. Ibid xiii.

18. Head "Some" 30.

19. Head *Serowe* xii.

20. Her assimilation to Botswana society was clearly only partial:

> "I have liked Botswana very much although I have got nothing out of having a country that didn't want me. Nobody here cares a damn if you like them or not. As far as a writer is concerned, you look a bit above mankind and mankind's prejudices and mankind's narrowness" (Marquard 52).

21. Head *Serowe* ix-x.

22. Ibid x.

23. Ibid 179.

24. Head "Some" 30.

25. Head has said "I do not have to be a feminist. The world of the intellect is impersonal, sexless." ("Writing Out of Southern Africa" in *New Statesman*, vol. 22). Her position inside the fiction is more complex, as *The Collector of Treasures* (1977) shows. See also Susan Gardner, "Production under Drought Conditions," *Africa Insight*, vol. 15, no. 1, 1985, pp.43-46.

26. *A Bewitched Crossroad* differs from Sol. T. Plaatje's *Mhudi* (edited by Tim Couzens, Quagga Press, 1975), and from Peter Abrahams's *Wild Conquest* (Faber, 1951), which cover some of the same historical ground, in that they seem to belong to the category of "historical romance," to be dramatizing the inner life of Southern African clashes in a range of representative characters, whereas Head is offering a very accurately researched historical study of Bechuanaland/Botswana which contains a lightly fictionalized central consciousness, and which uses some of the methods of fictional narratives.

27. Head seems to have developed this idea while working on *Serowe; Village of the Rain Wind*: "When I interviewed people I shaped the interviews in a certain way. I said to myself that Serowe is 73 years old and that is the life-span of one old man" (Marquard 50). Behind all the "lives" in Serowe is the shape of one long life. This device is more epically and lyrically deployed in *A Bewitched Crossroad*. Compare historian Barbara Tuchman's illuminating use of a representative life in her acclaimed study of the middle ages, *A Distant Mirror* (Penguin, 1978).

28. See the story "Heaven is Not Closed" in *The Collector of Treasures*.

29. Head *Serowe* xv.

30. Ibid xiv.

31. Head *Bewitched* 156.

32. Ibid 171.

33. Ibid 166.

34. Ibid 100.

35. In the tradition of "white" South African literature, this perception of black women has been founded on a sense of white sterility and evanescence in Africa, as opposed to an organic union with nature represented by a silent, traditional black woman. A classic locus is the closing scene of Olive Schreiner's *The Story of an African Farm*, in which Waldo, the young white male protagonist, dies against a backdrop of serene farm activity: "Near the shadow at the gable the mother of the little nigger stood churning. Slowly she raised and let fall the stick in her hands, murmuring to herself a sleepy chant such as her people love; it sounded like the humming of far-off bees" (273).

36. See Christopher Heywood's illuminating discussion of this tradition in "Traditional Values in the Novels of Bessie Head" (in *Individual and Community in Commonwealth Literature*, edited by Daniel Massa, Malta University Press, 1979, pp. 12-19).

37. Head *Bewitched* 187.

38. Ibid 161.

39. Ibid 27.

40. See Nick Davis's "Narrative Composition and Spatial Memory" (in *Narrative: From Malory to Motion Pictures*, edited by Jeremy Hawthorn, Arnold, 1985, pp.25-40), for a rich and relevant discussion of ways of "landscaping" the text's "memorial impression" (31). One such organizing device, necessary in a text which has to convey such complex information as the movements of numerous African tribes, is the use of chapter epigraphs, which recur inside the chapter at a critical moment. Another is the use of prophecy which Davis mentions as connecting "over very large narrative distances" (31). Also, "the text's own visible segmentation, since this blocks out action in arrangements" (31) which are suggestive and significant.

41. Head *Bewitched* 23.

42. Davis 31.

43. The British feared that the missionary "road to the north" would be blocked if Kruger's Transvaal base linked up with Germany in South West Africa, thus permanently blocking Britain's access northward.

44. See Olive Schreiner's *Trooper Peter Halket of Mashonaland* (Ad Donker, 1974) and Elizabeth Longford, *Jameson's Raid, the Prelude to the Boer War* (Jonathan Ball, 1982).

45. "I spent a whole portion of my life in a country where it was impossible for black people to dream, so I know what that's like. I spent another portion in a country

where it is possible to dream and I have combined these two different experiences in my writing" ("Some Notes on Novel Writing" 31).

46. Head *Serowe* xiv.

47. See, for instance, Dorothea Fairbridge, *A History of South Africa* (Oxford University Press, 1918): "Before leaving South Africa he gave himself eight months in an ox-wagon trekking in solitude through Bechuanaland and the Transvaal, reading Marcus Aurelius and Aristotle, dreaming his dreams of the future of the fair land of South Africa as one great self-governing dominion within the British Empire" (263).

48. Foreword to Kuzwayo's *Call Me Woman*, xiii.

49. This issue, of fictional characters' inner life, particularly in the South African novel, has recently been debated by critics like Njabulo Ndebele, who argues against the mechanistic surface representation of some black protest fiction, such as Mbulelo Mzamane's *The Children of Soweto*, and pleads for "interiority concretely rendered." ("Turkish Tales and Some Thoughts on S.A. Fiction," *Staffrider*, vol. 6, no. 1, 1984, pp. 24-48.) Many of his points have been taken up and argued out in a theoretical framework by Nick Visser, ("Victor Serge and the Poetics of Political Fiction," *Social Dynamics*, vol. 11, no. 2, 1985). Visser argues for a "socialized self" in radical fiction, and quotes E.P. Thompson's description of human experience as "persons experiencing their determinate productive situations and relationships.... and then "handling" this experience within their consciousness and their culture... and then acting upon their determinate situations in their turn" (quoted from *The Poverty of Theory* by Visser, p. 18). Bessie Head seems to achieve such a treatment of individuals in her fiction.

50. See, for instance, William Charles Scully's *A History of South Africa* (Longman, Green, 1922):

> One of the hinges, to use Froude's phrase, in the history of South Africa, is what is known as the "Great Trek," that migration of some 10,000 Europeans from the sparsely-peopled Cape Colony to the unknown north – to regions occupied only by wandering hordes of savages and wild animals (153).

See also Francis Carey Slater's *The Trek* (Macmillan, 1938), a long poem:

> On and on, to the unmapped spaces,
> Onward, in search of the hidden-places,
> Past lion's lair and leopard's den
> And swarming legions of savage men,
> On to the Land of the Trekker's dream,
> Where milk and honey in splendour stream:
> As an albatross over endless foam
> On-to discover the heart's own home !
> And Just-so, ho-ho, steady and slow,
> Onward the wagons go (6).

More recent South African history has also worked correctively to provide a more detailed picture of Southern African encounters between Boers, Blacks and the British. See, for instance Peter Delius, *The Land Belongs to Us* (Ravan, 1983).

51. Head *Bewitched* 163.

52. Ibid.

53. Ibid 31.

54. See Collingwood (219) who says that this is true "but in a sense not always recognized. It is the historian himself who stands at the bar of judgment, and there reveals his own mind in its strength and weakness, its virtues and its vices." Bessie Head emerges well from this test.

55. Head *Collector* 10.

56. Collingwood 233.

Olive Schreiner and Katherine Mansfield: Transformations of the Outcast Figure by Two Colonial Writers

The question underlying this paper is whether women writers in exile constitute a distinct and useful critical category.[1] Does the colonial woman writer in exile reconstitute her homeland, and her identity, in a distinctive way in her fiction, and what are the literal and emotional circumstances which she needs in order to create at all? I've tried to explore some of the parallels in Schreiner and Mansfield's life and art in order to construct a partial answer to these related questions. The "stories" I've concentrated on are Schreiner's "Prelude" to her big, unfinished novel, *From Man to Man*, written in 1888/89 at Alassio and Menton, and Mansfield's "Prelude", "At the Bay" and "The Voyage". Mansfield's "Prelude", begun when she was alone in Paris in March 1915, as "The Aloe" – "The Muses descended in a ring...and I fell into the open arms of my first novel"[2] – was continued in Bandol, in early 1916, during a happy and productive time with Middleton Murry, after her brother's death. "At the Bay", another of the "buds" of "The Aloe",[3] and "The Voyage" both belong (together with "The Doll's House" and "The Garden Party") to another period of intense creative activity, spent with Murry in Switzerland from July to October 1921. "A Married Man's Story" also belongs to this latter period, and seems to be a disguised comment on the bargain the woman writer often has to strike in order for art to happen at all.

For both writers, then, the works I'm considering arose in a period of intense and happy creativity; they themselves valued them as their best work; they were forms of "possession" – "as good as I can do, and all my heart and soul is in it"[4] – in which they created new forms which are yet an unfolding of their artistic individuality, reaching far back into early childhood, to their original colonial homes.

For both Schreiner and Mansfield, their actual relationship with the "mother country" was as fraught and ambivalent as their relationship with their own mothers, and with themselves. Arriving as disappointing substitutes for either dead or hoped for male children,[5] they experienced their mothers as unloving and punitive. Schreiner said of the two great whippings her mother gave her – for saying a word in Dutch, and for standing in a doorway catching raindrops – that the "immense harm" they did permanently influenced her life.[6] Mansfield described her mother as "cold as steel," and, indeed, the woman who eventually spies her married and pregnant daughter at the edge of a crowd after an absence of some years, tells her she looks "an old woman" and advises her to give her hat to the chambermaid, cannot be described as a fount of maternal affection.[7]

Similarly, the mother country was a place to escape from, a country of "lower middle-class Philistines"[8] with no aesthetic sense, imprisoning and fatal to the artist and the young woman. Personal freedom and artistic growth would be found elsewhere, in England, which they both called "Home". The bourgeoisie, the parental nuclear family, the conventional colonial fate for young womn, marriage and childbirth, were all resolutely opposed, rejected, and identified with the colony. Their early stories satirize German and Dutch (Afrikaner) stolidity, traditional participation in community rituals, anti-intellectualism, an unthinking participation in the cycle of "nature" – birth, procreation, and death. They exercise their humour on physical grossness, and cut their linguistic and satirical teeth on transliterations of Cape Dutch and German into ludicrous English. Their young female protagonists are detached outsiders, superior refined beings, who, elf-in-like, must have been exchanged at birth, or deserve kidnapping to a more exotic place.[9]

They are the pathetic victims of brutal and repressive adults who represent a brutal and repressive society – *The Story of an African Farm, In a German Pension*. Children are lashed for minor misdemeanours, young women are sexually harassed or seduced, babies are repulsive reminders of the realities of sex, which are either evaded for a higher, spiritual comradeship, or approached in outright fear, disgust, and loathing. In Mansfield's "The Child-Who-Was-Tired",[10] the exploited child/servant/victim dreams of escape and finds it by smothering the Frau's baby: he struggled "like a duck with its head off, wriggling." In Schreiner's "Dream Life and Real Life",[11] little Jannita, also a slave child labourer, flees her harsh employers after a flogging, but is herself killed while returning to warn them of an impending attack on the farmhouse. Waldo is flogged in *African Farm*, Lyndall, deprived of any "real" education, is seduced and abandoned by the father of her child, and dies after the death of her own baby. Mansfield's *In a German Pension* carries a strong thread of hysteria, which structures its artistic crises: at the conclusion of "At Lehmann's" the young girl's shriek at a first sexual advance, "breathing like a frightened little animal", coincides with the "frightful tearing shriek" of Frau Lehmann giving birth overhead.[12] Frau Brechenmacher, going to bed after the day's wedding party, "lay down...and put her arm across her face like a child who expected to be hurt as Herr Brechenmacher lurched in."[13] Sexuality and death often fuse at the artistic crisis of a story: at the end of "The Woman at the Store" an unpleasant little girl unveils her obscene, secret drawing, which is not the anticipated dirty picture but a view of her mother murdering her father.[14] Similarly, Mansfield's Journal entry concerning her first sexual experience with a man has "a flock of sheep passing down the street in the moonlight ...and behind, the dark, heavy cart – like a death cart... and all in this sacrificial light I look lovely."[15]

Though both Schreiner and Mansfield articulated a feminist creed for the artist – "we are firmly held with the self-fashioned chains of slavery"[16] – their craving for "experience" led them into a destructive series of personal traumas – phantom and real marriages, pregnancies, miscarriages and abortions – which were emotionally sterile and physically damaging. They were both troubled by guilt and threatening mental instability at so flagrantly transgressing their society's taboos. The illnesses which overtook them – Schreiner's asthma began at the conjunction of homelessness, family "rejection" and first sexual experience at 16, and Mansfield's tuberculosis superseded a long spell of other, less precise forms of ill-health – were deeply interwoven with a sense of personal failure, and personal flight from emotional difficulties. Both of them travelled restlessly from place to place after their initial break with the colony, living in hotels, boardinghouses, and temporary "homes".[17] Any "home", once set up, became a possible site of personal suffocation – Schreiner's "asthma" was both cause and effect of this lifelong caravanserai – and a place where the artist could not function and had to flee into solitude.[18] Solitude itself was ambivalent: it brought peace for a while, sometimes the ability to write, but soon, deepened into a terrifying loneliness.

Exile, then, was both physical situation and personal metaphor. The metropolitan "home", which offered an artistic centre, the literary life, the patronage of Arthur Symons and Oscar Wilde, the cult of the mask, a cultivated audience and venues for publication, also brought invasive hangers-on, sheer pressure of human numbers, and an alien landscape and climate in which the artist could not thrive: "It's so hard", writes Schreiner, "to paint that bright African world with this dark wild world about me."[19] Exile seemed to deepen the split between a creative artistic self, experienced as male, and a totally vulnerable female self.[20] In the first phase of exile, both women reveal a masochistic strain in their relationships with "strange" men. Schreiner told Havelock Ellis in 1885, of a man she'd had a brief love affair with: "I would like him to tread on me and stamp me fine into powder."[21] Mansfield, "smiling at myself", describes her infatuation with a certain "R" on board ship when travelling back to New Zealand in 1906, via Cape Town (where they landed a case of smallpox, and where she did not see Olive Schreiner on the quay, who was not about to leave for England): "When I am with him a preposterous desire seizes me, I want to be badly hurt by him. I should like to be strangled by his firm hands..." "All perfectly normal and healthy", comments one biographer, "especially the strangling part."[22]

Though both writers speak of art as an escape from self, a way of experiencing many different lives through "impersonation",[23] "mimicry" and "acting" (Lyndall, in *African Farm,* articulates this desire), their earlier repeated focus is on the child/woman as outcast and victim. Moreover, they were both good mimics of certain metropolitan modes. Schreiner's dream allegories on socialist and philosophical truths were written under Symbolist influence in the 1880's, published by Wilde, and ecstatically reviewed by Arthur Symons.[24] Mansfield wrote satirical sketches for *The New Age,* exercises in the pathos of class outcasts, and "marriage a la mode", while feeling, like Beryl in "Prelude", that the self who wrote in this manner was a false and superficial self, one who bored and rather disgusted "her real self".[25] The theme which at first claims their intensity is the vulnerability of the woman alone, especially the woman travelling alone, beyond the boundaries of a known world and a secure respectability. In Schreiner's *Undine* a young governess is on board ship to Africa; in *African Farm* Lyndall's outward journey into the Transvaal towards a point of destitution is partly healed by her return journey towards a Karoo mountain. In *The Little Governess* the protagonist journeys towards sexual betrayal by a "kindly grandpapa", one of a series of harassments by porters, gross young male travellers, and the final, triumphant waiter who celebrates her misfortune. "The Little Governess" is a finely mediated fictional fulcrum for both writers: written by a young woman from New Zealand sent to Queen's College, a charitable project of the Governesses' Benevolent Institution, it fictionalizes the social and sexual insecurity of any colonial girl travelling in Europe, and the real-life experiences of a South African governess. Here is a desperate journal entry, a message-in-a-bottle never sent, scrawled in pencil by Schreiner when travelling from England to Italy in 1887.

> I am here all alone in a train with a terrible Frenchman who I am sure is mad, and who I think means to attack me. I am going to throw this book out of the window if he does, that someone may find it. My address in England is New College, Eastbourne, England. This will be a most terrible night to me, even if nothing happens. We do not stop again till we get to Bale [sic]. He is sitting opposite me now trying to put his foot against mine. He would come and wrap my rug around me and put my hat on, and I dare not speak to him lest he should fly at me. I have never seen such a terrible face, handsome but with the awful look of one of the men in Balzac's novels. He is sitting now with his eyes *fixed* on me, I dare not look up or leave off writing. I've never felt such horror of any *human creature*. Oh God, if the train would stop. There's not any kind of bell one can pull. There ought to be things of some kind one can pull. He turns away to rub the glass of the window and peep out as if to see. We are passing *nothing*. I *hate* Frenchmen. He's a tall slight man, but fearfully strong. His hands could hold me like a little child. If he was an Englishman, I would talk with him and get command of him. We are just passing Aix-la-Chapelle. He has just caught hold of my hair. He says he always thought all English women wore bands. Oh God, oh God, what shall I do. I'm so afraid he's mad like that other man in the train. He is catching hold of my cloak and presses his face up to mine and says he likes me. I only shake my head and say I don't understand Frenchmen. Oh, perhaps we stop and he

will have to get out. The minute we stop, out I leap. I have opened the window and am sitting by it that if he touches me I can open it and leap out.[26]

Out of the nettle, danger, both women began to pluck the flower, art, but the figures granted some form of freedom and escape are at first only male. In *African Farm* it is Waldo who works through a crisis of faith and personal loss towards serenity. In Mansfield's "The Escape", concluding story to the volume *Bliss*, it is the husband who is granted the epiphany of the tree "an immense tree with a round, thick, silver stem and a great arc of copper leaves that gave back the light and yet were sombre." At the end of his train journey, he hears a woman singing, "something stirred in his breast... until he felt himself enfolded"; the vision irradiates his journey: "so great was his heavenly happiness...he wished he might live for ever."[27] In the title story, structural opposite to "The Escape" Bertha's vision of the "lovely pear tree" is sardonic, mocking her shattered life and fantasy.

Where, then, does the adult woman escape, for Mansfield and Schreiner? Is she ever granted this "flowering of the self, a self which is continuous and permanent – flowering for one moment upon the earth, most ourselves and least personal"?[28] For an answer to that question, we must turn away from England, as they both did, to the coast of France and Italy, and to Switzerland, where they went in search of physical and emotional health, and of the conditions in which to write. Landscape and climate were instantly closer to "home": "I like this place. I like this room. I like this sea. I like this sky, "writes Schreiner at Alassio in 1887, "I like these olive trees, they are like the "bush" at Ganna Iloek. It's like the Cape altogether... Nothing is walled off."[29] Soon after leaving England for France in 1915, Mansfield writes of her liking for the South of France: "For one thing, and it's awfully important, the sea is here – very clear and very blue... I shall be able to write here – in a day or two."[30] A little later she is walking "round by the sea towards St Cyr (which is very beautiful and wild and like my NZ)... My work is shaping for the first time today – I feel nearer it. I can see the people walking on the shore and the flowery clusters hanging on the trees."[31] This simulated "home" landscape combined a kind of security with a kind of freedom: it was enough like home to make a bridge into the remembered home artistically possible, to facilitate the memory's return, and yet sufficiently unlike home to enable the free artistic reconstruction to take place. Both women position themselves ritualistically within that landscape. Schreiner finds a ruined chapel at Santa Croce, "with the blue sky for a roof,"[32] a place combining the height and spiritual serenity of her early mission station environment with a recognizable landscape. She finds a terraced garden in an Alassio hotel which she makes her "walking-up-and-down place";[33] she had always composed and painted scenes while walking in a rocky place, a fairly enclosed area. Mansfield knows that France quickens her impressionistic talent, her ability to render a speedy, sensational life; she knows, too, that having registered those vivid impressions, she needs solitude: "To air oneself among these things, to seek them, to explore them and then to go apart and detach oneself from them – and to write – after the ferment has quite subsided."[34] Her space was even more cramped than Schreiner's: "I am now so tied and bound so caged that I know I'll sing."[35] The exterior space they required for creativity combines freedom and enclosure, familiarity and newness. As Schreiner wrote of the Karoo later: "It's like having a home of your own without the trouble of looking after it."[36] This telling domestic image raises the other, inner way in which both women seem to need to position themselves in relation to marriage or a family structure.

Schreiner's "Prelude" "flashed" on her, practically complete; once written, she discovered it was "a picture in small, a kind of allegory" of the life of her novel's main character, Rebekah.[37] Subtitled "The Child's Day", it recounts a long day, from dawn to dusk, as experienced by the 5-year-old Rebekah (a biblical name, like Kezia), a day on which her younger sister is born, the live twin of two girl babies. Schreiner's own sister, Ellie, had died at the age of 2 when Schreiner was 10, a crucial event for her emotionally and spiritually.[38] The protective love she felt for her coloured her sympathy for other women and "made a free-thinker" of her. Death lost its terrors, and so did Calvinist orthodoxy. In "Prelude", the little girl at first rejects the new-born sister who so engrosses her mother's attention, wanders about the farm, finds the dead baby in the spare room, adopts it and brings it her treasures, is chased away and told the truth about this baby, wanders in the lush garden, tells herself and an imaginary baby many stories and, finally, hearing the live baby cry out, goes in and insists on sleeping with it. Her fantasized mothering and gift-giving enable the real sibling bonding to take place. Rebekah is the little girl as artist:[39] imaginative activity releases family love; family love empowers the artist. The story reads like an allegory of Mansfield's own situation: the death of her brother Leslie in 1915 released her protective childhood feelings for him and for the world they'd shared as children. By drawing her dead brother emotionally, in fantasy, into her relationship with Murry, calling Murry by his pet-name, Bogey, she was able to "enter into her loss"[40] and make it a gain, to attach the newly awakened family affection to her adult sexual partner. This, in turn, seems to have enabled her to live with Murry and writer her finest stories in the latter half of 1921. The "bad karma" of fraudulent family figures masking real-life seducers, as in *The Little Governess*, is reversed: love of her brother, and the recollected, or at least posited, maternal affection of her mother for him, flooded her relationship with her male partner, her country, and the rejected girl-self originally identified and rejected with that country.

In Mansfield's "Prelude" the narcissistic doubling of mirror-images,[41] the dualism which afflicts female identity, is resolved by the active and mediating little girl Kezia, who carries the lamp of art[42] into the new house, and by the sympathetic pairing of female figures around the aloe: Mrs Fairfield and Linda regard it in the moonlight, Kezia and Linda by day. The aloe itself is both male and female, nature and artefact, a threatening plant and a fantasized vehicle of escape, riding on the grassy bank "like a ship with the oars lifted."[43] The grandmother's anticipated death can be cancelled in a game between her and Kezia; the brutal killing of a duck is forgotten as Kezia gazes up at the "killer" a man who, charmingly, is discovered to wear ear-rings. Male and female, life and death, constriction and freedom are shaped, contrasted and fused within a shifting, impersonal consciousness which is, and is not, that ot the little Kezia inside the story. This self-cancelling, self-delighting structure flows from the self-possession of Mansfield's mature art, which demands, like love, humility, and self-surrender.[44] "Like all great acts, it is pure risk."[45] In "At the Bay", too, Kezia and Linda are constantly linked. Linda is given the first stirrings of maternal feeling which were Mansfield's own towards her brother: the whole story is surrounded by the sea and the cycle of life, of which it is an endless miniature. Movements towards safety and danger oppose each other: the story could end either way, because the real life of action is endlessly repeatable; only art holds it momentarily in stasis. In "The Voyage", a journey by sea reverses the direction of the train journey in "The Little Governess": the movement is from loss to security, the boat-trip a sea-change of profound emotional importance. Here, loss heralds even greater security: the little girl carries her grandmother's totem swan-headed umbrella all the way from shore to shore, and it mutates into the live head of her grandpa, a "very old, wide-awake bird" as the swan-necked umbrella is hooked over the bed-rail.[46]

In these works, then, there is enough real integration "on the ground" for the further psychic integration, artistic recall, and form-giving activity,[47] to take place. The plight of the exiled woman, which is an extreme form of the plight of all women, as they seek an integration of the duality they struggle with, the split position which a patriarchal culture offers them as unconscious self-image,[48] is resolved through an art which builds a psychic bridge from the mature "male" artist to the young girl child at the heart of the story, who was once themselves. In this process, they also rejoin their countries of origin from a position of isolation outside it. Schreiner and Mansfield use strikingly similar images of isolation and community to describe the artistic process. Art expresses, writes Schreiner:

> the real self, that lives always in loneliness.

> Art is the little crack in the iron wall of life which shuts one in in awful isolation through which the spirit can force itself out and show itself to its own like-minded spirits outside: or rather can creep in through the cracks in their terrible walls that shut in the individual life and say, "You are not alone."[49]

The little girl in Schreiner's "Prelude" plays with a candle-flame, finding out how shifts in her vision and hand-movements can alter light and shadow, discovering a medium by which reality can be transformed and contained.[50] In "The Married Man's Story" the writer recalls playing with a candle-flame as a child, making a small wax lake, then sealing up the walls, controlling the release wax. An experience of "utter dreariness" is entered into and then conquered:

> The barriers are down. I had been all my life a little out-cast; but until that moment no-one had "accepted" me; I had lain in the cupboard – or the cave Forlorn... I did not consciously turn away from the world

86

of human beings; I had never known it; but I from that night did beyond words consciously turn towards my silent brothers...[51]

Women can never be pure objects of exchange in a kinship system; they have the power of words.[52] Driven ever deeper into the isolation that their fate as women artists decreed and, as artists in exile, intensified, what they developed in exile was the artistic power to spring the locks of their own prison. Their "flowering" was within the simulated world of art, not within the "real" world from whose natural benefits they often felt themselves shut out,[53] and yet, as Mansfield insists, art is "an attempt to create her own world *in* this world" and so *is* a part of reality, though reality "cannot become the ideal, the dream."[54] Murry echoes Mansfield here, in a letter to Sarah Gertrude Millin:

> Art isn't the expression of an idea, but of a life – and what's more, it is the only complete expression of life, it's the only way life can perfectly and completely express itself.[55]

Identity is formed in alienation, and alienation from "home" seems to have been one of the springs of Schreiner and Mansfield's best artistic work.[56] Schreiner returned to South Africa in 1880 but her writing then became subservient to immediate political issues and social pressures. Yet Mansfield continued to feel that her separation from her country had been an irreparable loss. In her last years she wrote to Sarah Gertrude Millin:

> ...I am sure it does a writer no good to be transplanted – It does harm. One reaps the glittering top of the field but there are no sheaves to bind... I think the only way to live as a writer is to draw upon one's own real familiar life – to find the treasure in that as Olive Schreiner did. Our secret life, the life we return to over and over again, the "do you remember" life is always the past. And the curious thing is that if we describe this which seems to us so intensely personal, other people take it to themselves and understand it as if it were their own.[57]

Notes

1. For the purposes of this discussion, I'm ignoring the (false) assumption that Schreiner wrote her best work before leaving South Africa in 1881, at the age of 26. Parts of *From Man to Man* (Fisher Unwin, 1926), the novel she reinvented and revised for the rest of her life, and especially the "Prelude" to it, surpass *African Farm* (1883) in imaginative conception, execution, and maturity of vision.

2. Letter to J.M. Murry, 24 March 1915, *The Collected Letters of Katherine Mansfield* vol. 1, edited by W. O'Sullivan and Margaret. Scott, Clarendon Press, 1984, p.167. "Prelude" emerged from "The Aloe" in 1917; see Antony Alpers, *The Life of Katherine Mansfield* (Oxford University Press, 1982, p.178).

3. See *The Collected Letters*, pp.348-349, for evidence that "At the Bay" was also creatively rooted in "The Aloe", conceived as a "novel" about childhood in New Zealand. Mansfield calls it "A continuation of "Prelude", see C.K. Stead, *The Letters and Journals of Katherine Mansfield* (Allen Lane, 1977, p. 232).

4. See K. Mansfield, Letter to the Hon. Dorothy Brett, September 1921 (in C.K. Stead's *Letters and Journals*, p.232). She describes "The Voyage" as a "kind of possession" in a letter to William Gerhardi, 13 March 1922, *Letters and Journals*, p.258. Schreiner sent her "Prelude" to all her close friends, said she liked it "the best of all the things I have written" (Richard Rive, editor, *Olive Schreiner: Letters 1871-99*, David Philip, 1987, p. 339) and after completing it she "lay and slept on the top of a hill near Menton half in a sweet dream kind of way with joy that my Prelude was done" (Rive *Letters* 149).

5. In the Schreiner family, three male siblings died in the years before Schreiner's own birth (on 24th March 1855) and she was given versions of their names, Emile, Albert, and Oliver: Olive Emilie Albertina Schreiner. Mansfield was the third of a family of girls until her brother, Leslie Heron Beauchamp, arrived. She often writes of a father's excited responses to the arrival of a male heir, and expresses a sense of her parents' "disappointment" in her. See also Alpers, p. 13.

6. See S.C. Cronwright-Schreiner, *The Life of Olive Schreiner* (T. Fisher Unwin, 1924, p. 250). A story of Mansfield's called "Sixpence" (*Collected Stories*, Constable, 1945, pp.678-684) also suggests that the effect of a childish beating is ineradicable, and cannot be "bought off", though "The Little Girl" (pp. 577-581) moves in an opposite direction, from punishment to the security of a father's embrace.

7. Alpers 94.

8. See S.C. Cronwright-Schreiner, *The Letters of Olive Schreiner* (T. Fisher Unwin, 1924, p. 183), and Stead's *Letters and Journals* (p.26), for Mansfield's comment: "When New Zealand is more artificial, she will give birth to an artist who can treat her natural beauties adequately."

9. Lyndall, in *African Farm*, is described in terms of elfin beauty, and Mansfield's story "How Pearl Button was kidnapped" is about a little girl's joyous adventure when kidnapped from "The House of Boxes".

10. Mansfield 757-765.

11. A story written in the same period as *African Farm*, first published in 1893 in *Dream Life and Real Life*, Unwin, Pseudonym Library.

12. Mansfield 742-743.

13. Ibid 725.

14. Ibid 572.

15. Alpers 59.

16. Ibid 61.

17. Mansfield had 29 postal addresses in London between 1908 and 1916 (Alpers 200-201); Schreiner moved even more often, both in Europe and South Africa. Sec also Stead, p.122.

18. See the *Collected Letters*, p.174, for one such moment in a recurring pattern for Mansfield: "I cannot write my book living in these two rooms" (with Murry in Notting Hill). See also letter to S.S. Koteliansky, 28 November 1815: "Don't believe the conjugal 'we'...it's not really true of me, never" (*Letters* 210).

19. Cronwright-Schreiner *Letters* 50.

20. See Alpers, p. 49: "I am a child, a woman, and more than half man." Schreiner often insisted that she was not "really" a woman; she uses scenes of cross-dressing (*African Farm*), and Rebekah in *From Man to Man* has an intense story/fantasy in which she is a husband lying next to a pregnant wife.

21. See Ellis's notes on Schreiner, Schreiner collection, Humanities Research Centre, Texas.

22. Alpers 40-41.

23. See Mansfield, Letter to Sylvia Payne, 24 April 1906: "Would you not like to try all sorts of lives – one is so very small – but that is the satisfaction of writing – one can impersonate so many people" (*Letters* 19). Lyndall, in *African Farm* likes to "realize forms of life utterly unlike mine" (201).

24. In *The Athenaum* Vol. 47 (10 January 1891); reprinted in C. Clayton, (cd.) *Olive Schreiner*, McGraw-Hill, 1983. pp.78-79.

25. "By dint of hiding from others the self that is within us – we may end by being unable to find it ourselves", wrote Mansfield (Alpers 72).

26. Cronwright-Schreiner *Life* 178.

27. Mansfield 201-202.

28. Stead 173.

29. Cronwright-Schreiner *Letters* 112-113.

30. O'Sullivan 201. Mansfield writes: "The muse waits on the edge of the sea" (Cronwright-Schreiner *Letters* 305).

31. O'Sullivan 205-206.

32. See her allegory "In a Ruined Chapel", published in *Dreams*, Unwin, 1890, which is set in the Alassio environment.

33. See, for instance, O'Sullivan p. 182, but in each new environment she sought or created such an outdoor walking area for "writing" in. Like Mansfield, she sometimes thought out stories in their entirety before "writing out". See Stead, p. 123: "I sit and think them out, and if I overcome my lassitude and do take the pen they ought (they are so word perfect) to write themselves."

34. O'Sullivan 288.

35. O'Sullivan 210.

36. Cronwright-Schreiner *Letters* 182.

37. Cronwright-Schreiner *Letters* 291.

38. Rive 113.

39. See Jean Marquard, "Olive Schreiner's 'Prelude': The Child as Artist" (*English Studies in Africa, vol. 22*, no. 1, 1979).

40. O'Sullivan 215.

41. Freud discusses doubling both in terms of a narcissistic phase (Beryl's mirror images) and originally as "an insurance against the destruction of the ego," an "energetic denial of the power of death". See Juliet Mitchell, *Psychoanalysis and Feminism*, Penguin, 1974, pp. 386-7. In this case the creative "doubling" of female identities in Kezia and Linda, mother and daughter, and in Schreiner's sisters, Rebekah and Bertie, would have the second function.

42. The lamp occurs again in "The Doll's House", a story which integrates the child outcast in the figure of "our Else". Kezia is again the mediator between authority and the "excluded" group in showing the "lamp" to Else (see Clare Hanson and Andrew Gurr, *Katherine Mansfield*, Macmillan, 1981, p. 128). This study provided a stimulus for many points in this paper). Mansfield associates the lamp with love, as well, in a letter to Garnett Trowell, 2 October 1908: "I picture us coming home at night... the shutter closed, the lamp on the open table – like the sun of a green world – you and I – the world shut out and yet the world in our power" (*Letters* 78).

43. Mansfield 53.

44. Stead 200, 234.

45. Alpers 330.

46. Mansfield 330.

47. Juliet Mitchell mentions Freud's idea of a dualism of drives: "the death-drive which impels towards repetition and conservation, and the sexual drive which pushes forward to the production of *new forms*" (390, my emphasis).

48. Mitchell offers an illuminating discussion of women's psychology within an analysis of patriarchy, and argues that Freud's psychoanalytic concept of the unconscious is a concept expressing mankind's transmission of a "father-dominated social structure" (402-403). There is no symmetry in the cultural making of men and women: though both male and female children "want to take the father's place"; only the boy is allowed to do so. "Furthermore, both sexes are born into the desire for the mother,... but only the boy can fully recognize himself in his mother's desire" (404). Thus both sexes repudiate the implications of femininity, which is "in part a repressed condition... and returns in symptoms such as hysteria." Mitchell's argument seems relevant to both Schreiner and Mansfield, who "recover" a "repressed" femininity in their best work.

49. Cronwright-Schreiner *Letters* 323.

50. Schreiner *Man* 66-67.

51. Mansfield 447.

52. See Mitchell on Levi-Strauss's discussion of women in kinship systems (371).

53. A striking example of this feeling, and yet an artistic skill in representing it, is found in Mansfield's letter to J.M. Murry, 7 May 1915 (*Letters* 177).

54. Stead 240-241.

55. Letter from J. Middleton Murry to S.G. Millin, 28th August 1926, Millin collection, William Cullen Library, University of the Witwatersrand, Johannesburg.

56. See Mitchell, p. 383ff: "The very self, the subject, is only created as a *difference.*" "Lack" also "sets in motion the movement forward" (386); thus, exile itself, the lack of the "home country sets in motion the desire to move towards it," in dream, fantasy (Mansfield's many dream voyages back to New Zealand) and in art.

57. Katherine Mansfield, letter to S.G. Millin, n.d. (dated by Millin's biographer, and internal evidence, as 1921), Millin collection.

White Settlers in the Heart of Empire: Visionary Power in Lessing's *The Four-Gated City*

The whole process of writing is a setting at a distance. That is the value of it... the process... takes the raw, the individual, the uncriticized, the un-examined, into the realm of the general. – (Lessing Under My Skin 397)

The slow living through the fifties really was like crawling up out of a pit. – (Lessing Walking in the Shade 358)

They alone shall possess the earth who live from the powers of the cosmos.
– Walter Benjamin

Doris Lessing describes the *Children of Violence* pentateuch as a bildungsroman cycle which explores the relationship between the individual conscience and the collective. She often speaks of herself, her heroine Martha, her contemporary cohorts, and her times as determined by the two world wars between which she was born, in 1919. The violence which amputated her father's leg, married him to his nurse, and helped to precipitate her parents' move to Southern Rhodesia in search of an alternative order – landownership, farming, and space, the colonial dream – seems to have determined the shape of her imagination and her fictional enterprise, which is tenacious and epic in reach as it seeks to reorder and heal the original violence. She says: "There is a pattern in my mind... where order breaks into disorder and extremity. It came from World War I and my parents' destruction by it." This pattern is also in others, "for we are not sufficient to ourselves."[1]

Lessing's fiction develops and strengthens this insight into the human need for something beyond the autonomy often celebrated in humanist or feminist creeds. Her parents' colonial dream in Southern Rhodesia did not lead to an opening out of their minds and lives, but rather to contraction, disappointment, and madness, the colonial paranoia which, in its racial form, engulfs her first protagonist, Mary Turner of *The Grass Is Singing*, and which remains a central theme in her fiction, because the divided identity of women is later revealed to be a condition of capitalist patriarchy in the West. Her parents' true lives were not lived in Africa but were nostalgically lived elsewhere, in Persia or England, in a lost past, or deferred to a future which would be lived elsewhere, perhaps in a regained England of their dreams. In her autobiographical writings, Lessing herself identifies the damaging nuclear family that she knew, and responded to with anger and rebellion, as coterminous with a closed, racially ordered colonial society. The family is shown to be the microcosm of that colonial settler society. Much of her fiction seems to renegotiate the terms between individual and collective in order to glean some new understanding of the workings of power, knowledge, consciousness, and identity by constructing complex narrative patterns that interweave documentary and fantasy modes.

In this fictional reordering of space, lives, events, history, and houses, women's lives play a crucial role. As Nicole Ward Jouvé has pointed out, "the particular 'situation' or 'position' of women is continuously at stake in her novels."[2] Lessing drives the precariousness of women's position under capitalist patriarchy to an extreme, often by testing and strengthening it against unreason, madness, altered states of mind, insight, telepathy, and prophecy. In doing this she is not exalting irrationality or celebrating woman as telepathic goddess, but calling into question the whole Western enterprise of scientific rationality as a defining element in that feudal, patriarchal Eurocentric order which was transported to the colonies and which subordinates women by dividing them into separate functions that serve the male order: hostess, legal wife, sexual partner, biological mother, surrogate mother, secretary. There is a proliferation of roles for women, particularly in *The Four-Gated City*, which, like Atwood's *Handmaid's Tale*, draws attention to the social construction of womanhood by separating female functions into different bodies or groups serving one man or class of men. The inability of any one woman to be whole and individual indicts the social system of which she is a part, while the relationships between individual women or groups of women stress different but related forms of subordination.

And yet *The Four-Gated City* is also a novel about the quest of the protagonist, Martha, to make her own accommodation with England, more particularly the sprawling city of London, the heart of Empire, as a newly arrived colonial woman who has left two marriages-husbands and children-behind her. Like Joseph Conrad's *Heart of Darkness*, the novel opens around the Thames estuary, in a world both closed off by the class system and yet severely damaged by the bombs of the Second World War. Leaving "home" to come "home"[3], Martha discovers that the darkness that sent out the civilizing mission to Africa is also here. Yet here, too, is the detailed memory of the working-class women in the locality, a "section map in depth".[4] Transactions between women become a counterforce to the separations inflicted by the class system, patriarchy, the geography of London, and a traditional feudal domestic economy. This is one of the forms that Doris Lessing's feminist insights take, and she reveals how class alliances can foster an understanding of gender construction and class differences, as Martha Quest tries to avoid the matchmaking schemes of her working-class friends. Later in Martha's stay in London, she is taken up in a form of intense transactional analysis in the relationship of the main three protagonists, the always shifting, long maintained ménage à trois which is the defining condition of Western social neurosis but also the symbolic vehicle of its cure. New forms of love, desire, sharing, and spirituality come out of the complex emotional and psychological transactions that occur with Lynda, Mark, and Martha as the nucleus, but which have ripple effects on their close circle of friends. This growth within the triangular desire of the nuclear family then fans out in the latter part of the novel into a wider understanding of the relationship between empires and colonies, and the family structures that mediate cultural blindness and insight.

The Four-Gated City does a lot of complex therapeutic and cultural work around the concepts of the family, confinement, madness, colonialism, and violence.[5] It constantly denaturalizes the family and gender roles, thus showing them up as a "contingent rather than necessary system of practices".[6] Asymmetrical, unconventional, and surrogate families extend across three generations and seem to be a proliferating reply to Lessing's colonial nuclear family of origin, in which a frigid woman nursed a mutilated man, and its equally sick metropolitan antecedent, in which a fragmenting Englishman of the upper middle class nurses a mad, frigid wife who is sometimes in a mental hospital, sometimes in the basement with a Grace Poole-type warden.[7] The pattern of Victorian fiction, described by Sandra Gilbert and Susan Gubar as the repression and projection of rage onto a confined Other, a Madwoman in the Attic, and redescribed by Gayatri Spivak as the Western woman's consolidation of ego and authority over the body of a colonized woman, takes a new twist or a reversal in *The Four-Gated City*. Bertha Mason has come to London from Zambesia to nurse Virginia Woolf. In this process she herself almost goes mad, but rescues herself by conducting mescaline experiments to test the limits of her own consciousness. In these experiments the repressed violent side of liberalism manifests itself in vision, as the binaries and hatreds of anti-Semitism, racism, feudalism, and sexual hierarchy march through Martha's consciousness.[8]

These experiments take courage, in fiction as in life, and involve suffering. The experiments in vision and madness that Martha and Lynda undertake are what Lessing means when she speaks of evolution of consciousness, an evolution into a realm consistently denigrated by Western rationality, but one that offers forms of healing to Lynda and Martha as they struggle with their lives of mental and emotional confinement. Martha develops forms of prophecy and telepathy: the forms of new understanding she develops in conjunction with Lynda entitle them to be the heroes of the new order that develops in the communalist, futuristic realm depicted in the Epilogue as a counter-response to an age of nuclear warfare. The complex and detailed depiction of their struggle to communicate with one another is moving and rich, representing as it does every woman's attempt to escape her social conditioning into separation and subordination. It represents more than that, though: it reveals the way in which the class system, patriarchy, colonialism, and Western rationalism are mutually articulated and reinforcing.[9] Forms of knowledge are articulated with forms of power: the inner power both women develop, using the levers of African and Eastern traditions, Sufi wisdom, antipsychiatry, and instinct, allow them to escape to a degree their confinement within "the psychic fantasy of woman," which splits women into idealized and denigrated aspects, and which is the foundational fantasy of the patriarchal capitalist order (Brennan).

The psychic experiments in the basement, as Lynda taps her bloodied fingertips around the walls, are the individual counterpart in the narrative of the broad socialist movement of the British Left toward the Aldermaston antinuclear marches of the early 1960s (marvellously rendered in a historically synoptic chapter in Part 3) and represent its subterranean gender component. As Lessing says, the tension between the individual and the collective is the great subject of her novel sequence, and *The Four-Gated City* gives that tension epic form: individuals are shown animating broad social movements, drawn in by them, rejecting the Communist Party, suffering mental breakdowns, committing suicide in the wake of Cold War defections to the West, divorcing, reconnecting, giving dinner parties, making up layered collages of their past on the walls, endlessly discussing people and ideas, trying to understand and help their damaged children. The private costs of public involvements are shown, and are worked through in some way, in dialogue and ritual, in the retrospective discoveries and anticipatory hypotheses that people conduct in their own lives and the lives of others.

It has been argued that Lessing's work suffers from her move toward representative characters (Weinhouse), that fiction begins to be starved out by philosophy (Thorpe), that her vision of women as the nurturers of a new race does not connect with a feminist need for equality in work and relationships (Christ). I would argue that the broad canvas of *The Four-Gated City*, its constant movement between public and private, the spectrum of characterization between individual and type, and more especially the dialogue it sets up between colony and metropolis as characters circulate between Africa and England, not least in Martha's gradual evolution into a semi-assimilated Englishwoman, reveals that the defining conditions of colonialism and gender relations are similar and are historically interconnected. Fanon writes, in rebuttal of Mannoni, that "European civilization and its best representatives are responsible for colonial racism,"[10], not a special group or subclass of Europeans, which has often been an implicit or explicit assumption in discussions of colonialism. Martha has a vision of this in her tranced state in Paul's room, a trance she enters, like the San (Bushman) rock artists of southern Africa, to gain further insight after her dialogues with the "mad" Englishwoman, Lynda. To quote Fanon again: "there are inner relationships between consciousness and the social context."[11] He also quotes Pierre Naville: "it is the economic and social conditions of class conflicts that explain and determine the real conditions in which individual sexuality expresses itself."[12]

Almost every scene of sexual relationship in the novel expresses some form of alienation: narcissism, control, degradation, cruelty, subordination. It is as if the early extreme form of sexual collusion in paranoid racial fantasy, so graphically depicted in *The Grass Is Singing*, has been exchanged for myriad milder forms of aberration, the gender malaise which has succeeded the original matrix of imperialism. Margaret Coldridge has a homosexual husband; Martha has an initial sexual relationship with a war survivor (from a brutalized South African background) who seems at first to offer her sex as concentrated communication, but is juggling a timetable of female visitors and later becomes a perverted pimp and brothel-keeper; Lynda is frigid as a wife and a mother; the next generation seems to exchange the fantasy of sex for the fantasy of money or surrogate parenting, and are as caught in childish anti-parent rebellion as Martha and Mark. The ex-Communists see the conventional family as merely a myth to be exploded; the British public school system creates unhappy children without emotional resources. In short, the Western capitalist system and the world of global expansion and commodity markets have wreaked forms of distortion and corruption intertwined with the violent legacy of two world wars.

This is the world that Lessing depicts, with the critical eye of a semi-outsider, in the England of the 1950s and 1960s. At the turn of the decade she registers the transformation of an older Romantic Left into the commodified clothes- and food-conscious Cultural Left of the Swinging Sixties. She speaks of her desire to perform documentary functions in her fiction, to offer a chronicle of the times, to convey memory and knowledge. In *The Four-Gated City* she especially wanted to reach a younger audience, and in the novel Martha takes on the role of foster mother to the disturbed generation bred by Cold War defections, divorce, parental breakdown, and suicide. The fourth book of the novel, after Martha and the reader have travelled through a series of locks and openings (the sexual relationship with Jack; a breakdown caused by her mother's visit; a partnership with Mark and public involvement; her interior journey with Lynda and extended family parenting) moves toward a moment of self-acceptance in the here and now: "She thought, in the dove's voice of her solitude: Where? But where. How? Who? No, but where, where.... Then silence and the birth of a repetition: Where. Here. Here? Here, where else, you fool, you poor fool, where else has it been, ever."[13]

The Epilogue then further explodes the gradually unraveling time frames of the novel to depict a world of retreat into Primitive Communism, experimental lifestyles, and escape from a poisoned radioactive England after a Grand Catastrophe. The stage is being set for the space fictions that would follow. The omniscient narrator disappears, to be replaced by documentation, archives, letters between people now isolated from one another. It is as if the whole rotten edifice has to be destroyed so that small, new beginnings can occur. The journey of colonials to England is again reversed and Joseph, a young gardener of mixed race, is about to be sent by Martha to Nairobi, where Francis, Mark Coldridge's son, is now working as head of a rehabilitation centre. The particulars of colonial life have been absorbed by metropolitan life, then regurgitated, and are now in need of renewal from the Africa to which the original imperialists traveled. This expanded spatial consciousness and time frame create the mold of Lessing's space fictions, which would follow the *Children of Violence* sequence.

Joseph is one of the new children, raised within a new context. The explosion of England is a necessary fictional corollary of the insight.conveyed throughout the novel, that colonialism and war were created by a sickness within Europe, masked by civilization. New gardens are needed and Joseph, with his symbolic spiritual name, perhaps heralds an era of healing and reconciliation beyond the wars.

The Epilogue, in its new configuration of narrative, between myth and history, also sets the stage for what Lessing calls "the contrition of History".[14] This contrition is an epic form of the remorse that Martha's mother is described as feeling when she eventually has a friendship with an African boy and discovers that she has been fed racist lies all her life. The contrition of history is what Foucault seems to mean when he discusses the challenge that madness and creativity pose to society in general: "through madness, a work that seems to drown in the world... actually engages within itself the world's time, masters it, and leads it; by the madness which interrupts it, a work of art opens a void, a moment of silence, a question without answer, provokes a breach without reconciliation where the world is forced to question itself."[15]

This nexus of colonialism, racism, family, and madness is what *The Four-Gated City*, as the concluding volume of Martha Quest's *Bildung*, explores in depth, in many dimensions and idioms. As some critics have pointed out, the self-division of the characters is replicated in the narrative form: Martha is both narrating consciousness and chief actor (Whitlock). This doubleness can be seen as a richness and an instrumental strategy for healing in the symbolic realms.[16] Lessing as author is also Martha, and not Martha. The narrative form of this bildungsroman allows identification and disidentification, which gives a flexibility to female identity, one that is often disavowed in the actual plot sequence of forms of constraint and confinement. The same freedom is taken in passages of cultural analysis and documentary information, in which the novel abounds. This narrative flexibility and doubleness elude "the appropriating Narcissism of the West";[17] in fact it turns the colonial mirror of the West back upon itself. This double narrative consciousness, that of a colonial female self in search of an identity at the heart of Empire that turns into a labyrinth of power relations, both antecedent and contingent, is perhaps the novel's answer to Said's request for an "epistemological critique of the connection between a historicism which expands to include antithetical attitudes... and the actual practices of imperialism,"[18], for art and madness represent "a discovery of the central incertitude where the work of art is born".[19]. This central incertitude of art and madness which Lessing explores is counter-hegemonic. If postmodernism is "European culture's awareness that it is no longer the unquestioned and dominant centre of the world,"[20] then the dialogue that Lessing sets up between Europe and its Others (in Africa, America, and Russia), and the narrative consciousness that she uses to convey her vision in *The Four-Gated City* makes it a postmodern fiction.

What I have been arguing is that it is a postmodern fiction that serves postcolonial ends, in that it shows colonialism to exist within a nexus of global power relations, and at the heart of the human psyche, while constructing a fictional narrative that allows its protagonists to move toward moments of intercultural understanding, and compassion. In the space fiction that would follow, Lessing would reach and further create the new younger audience who are, in every generation, the redemption of the fallen world she so graphically describes in the *Children of Violence* sequence. The expanded spiritual, moral, and political consciousness that is needed to counter the degradation of Western capitalist environments is created within an audience of new readers.

Notes

1. Lessing *Walking* 268.

2. Jouvé 106.

3. Lessing *Four-Gated* 10.

4. Ibid.

5. Foucault illuminates the historical and literary traditions which undergird *The Four-Gated City* and the connections between patriarchy, power, and confinement in his *Madness and Civilization*: "The prestige of patriarchy is revived around madness in the bourgeois family" (286). Lessing uses madness in the novel to deconstruct that prestige.

6. Alcoff 11.

7. The intertextual references to *Jane Eyre* include the enigmatic first appearance of Mark Coldridge (his name a compendium of Brontë ruggedness, exposure, and the Cold War); the rumours about and gradual appearance of a mad wife; Martha's role as secretary and foster mother to Mark's child, Francis. The whole novel reworks the British paradigm of the *Jane Eyre* story from the colonial perspective while showing forms of continuity in domestic and political oppression.

8. Martha's vision of violence, hatred, and disturbance has many parallels with scenes in another Southern African novel of breakdown, Bessie Head's *A Question of Power*.

9 Teresa Brennan's discussion of these connections in *History After Lacan* is especially useful here. She draws out the historical and political implications of Lacan's theory of ego formation: there are "connections between the ego's era, ethnocentrism in a postcolonial context, ecological crisis, and the existence of ongoing war" (27).

10. Fanon 90-91.

11. Ibid 97.

12. Ibid 105.

13. Lessing *Four-Gated* 559.

14. Ibid 573.

15. Ibid 286.

16. I see this aspect of the narrative form as one answer to Jouvé's question in her provocative discussion of the *Children of Violence* sequence: what is the relation "between the authorial voice and the heroine who is devised as a mirror for authorial experience" (111).

17. Young 17.

18. Quoted in Young p. 10.

19. Foucault 286.

20. Young 19.

Family and State in Prison Narratives by South African Women

I want to use a group of prison narratives by South African women to contest some of the implications of the current terms "post-colonial", "post-apartheid" and "post-feminist". The "post prefix in all cases seems to suggest a movement beyond the struggles of the past, to describe an already existing or desired state beyond the dialectic of power struggles figured in the earlier terms "colonialism", "apartheid" and "feminism", which connoted sites of struggle organized around nationality, race, and gender. The assumption seems to be that those struggles have become dated and unnecessary, as we now live in an era in which a

> destructive cultural encounter is changing to an acceptance of differ-
> ence on equal terms. Both literary theorists and cultural historians are
> beginning to recognize cross-culturality as the potential termination
> point of an apparently endless human history of conquest and annihi-
> lation justified by the myth of group purity and as the basis on which
> the post-colonial world can be creatively stabilized.[1]

It is argued in this view that comparative methodology and the hybridized and syncretic view of the modern world which this implies[2] is the gateway to a new dispensation both in socio-political forms and critical methodology. This critical line often privileges texts which are themselves hybridized, syncretic, deconstructive and self-referential, such as those of Wilson Harris and J.M. Coetzee. Only texts which self-consciously deconstruct European "monoliths, which erode their own biases, are seen as offering liberation into a world in which one's own identity may be created or recuperated... as a process, a state of continual becoming in which both author/ity and domination of any kind is impossible to sustain."[3] These sets of analogies between political structures, literature and criticism are attractive but, I think, misleading in terms of the ways in which power structures and the shaping of identity in response to those power structures continue to operate in the "real" world. Prison writing offers us a model of a literature responding strongly, with all the resources of one particular, limited human identity, thrown back upon itself, to a particularly punitive expression of a given state's power to curb dissent (to limit discussion to political prisoners for the moment). Imprisonment can become a very flexible cosmic metaphor, but it is also a term for a physical incarceration of the body which can be conjugated with some variety through different societies, history and geography.[4] Though it punishes individuals, it must be seen, as Kenyan writer Ngugi wa Thiong'o argues, in the context of "the historical struggles of all people against economic, political and cultural slavery".[5] Ngugi's prison diary issues from postcolonial Kenya, thus indicating one of the first disjunctions in the terminology which equates "post-coloniality" with "freedom". He writes:

> A year as an inmate of Kamiti (prison) has taught me what should have been obvious; that the prison system is a repressive weapon in the hands of a ruling minority determined to ensure maximum security for its class dictatorship over the rest of the population and it is not a monopoly exclusive to South Africa and England.[6]

In the context of colonialism, imprisonment should also be seen as simply another inflection of the kind of control previously expressed in slavery and indentured labour.[7] As Lucy A. Delaney's nineteenth century slave narrative puts it, when she hears the key turn in the prison door:

> My only crime was seeking for that freedom which was my birthright! I heard Mr. Mitchell tell his wife that he did not believe in slavery, yet, through his instrumentality, I was shut away from the sunlight, because he was determined to prove me a slave, and thus keep me in bondage. Consistency, thou art a jewel![8]

The same point is made a century later by Caesarina Kona Makhoere, author of *No Child's Play: In Prison under Apartheid*, when she was imprisoned in South Africa after the school and township resistance of 1976 to the imposition of Afrikaans as language of instruction. She describes how black women prisoners are forced to wear the "doek" (headscarf) and apron, which symbolize their domestic servitude outside the prison. "We do not live in the daydreams of the apartheid gods" she writes.[9] Ngugi, too, places imprisonment in the context of resistance during both the colonial and post-colonial periods: "the first prerequisite for this resistance was a rejection of the slave consciousness contained in the colonial culture of imperialism."[10]

Imprisonment, then, tries to confirm the pattern of slavery by breaking those who dissent from it but, in doing so, it calls into being a further excited and resistant avowal of individual identity which is the best bulwark against domination and which, through an enforced isolation from the rest of humanity, forges in suffering new and stronger forms of solidarity with that community. Those who survive are stronger for knowing what ultimate abuses of power can inflict: prison, as Ruth First notes when she sees the names of former political prisoners scratched on the exercise yard door, is a place of reunion and an archive.[11] This roll of honour, chequered by human frailties, again suggests the intransigence of human identity: the first act a prisoner performs is to write his name on the cell wall.[12] The prison memoir, especially, is rooted in an individual resistant identity which feels itself to be in a special relationship with a historical collectivity and thus reminds us that literature is, as Barbara Harlow points out, a "political and politicized activity"[13] and that the history of colonial struggle is made up of acts of resistance which include writing about that struggle, whether or not the person who entered the prison was already a writer and was being punished for that form of permanent dissidence, permanent individuality. Prison seems to make even the reluctant writer, the activist into a writer: the difficulty of the task, the silence, call forth the activity. If toilet paper is the only paper, and cell walls the only blank surface, people inscribe on them the communications which cannot yet reach outward, to others.

To turn to the more complex relationship of the terms "post-apartheid" and "post-feminist", I want to consider briefly the role played by gender within South African prison narratives, and to examine some of the differences revealed in the negotiations between family and state which these narratives enact.

In South Africa, where the state has been so evidently and abusively built on racial classification and discrimination, the distinction between political and common-law crime becomes blurred, as Makhoere points out ("all prisoners, black and white, are political prisoners).[14] In a nondemocratic regime, all crimes become in themselves accusations: Rose Moss's novel, *The Schoolmaster*, based on the Johannesburg station bombing by John Harris, makes this case well in the courtroom scene, which often serves to articulate the moral basis of political "crime" in prison literature: "The law itself is criminal."[15] Makhoere feels solidarity in prison with domestic servants who have killed their white madams; Ellen Kuzwayo, a writer and social worker, also briefly detained, mentions how her attitudes toward juvenile crime have changed over the years of resistance.[16] The release of Mandela and other political prisoners, great event though it is, does not in itself usher in a post-apartheid regime, and even a post-apartheid regime may have prisons like Kenya's Kamiti prison.

In women's prison narratives the issue of the law becomes even more problematic. Women are natural outlaws, as Christina Stead tells us; they have to find themselves in complex negotiations around patriarchal laws in family and state. If the law is identified with the father, and the father is the one who is empowered both in family and state, how is the woman writer to attain to independence, power, and authorship? Women writers make complex affiliations with paternal roles and identities in their fiction, and the writing itself may enact an emancipatory or conservative trajectory (Olive Schreiner, S.G. Millin and Pauline Smith are all interesting here). But though prison is a place where a deep solidarity is forged be tween black and white (Hugh Lewin argues that only through prison experience can whites feel exactly what it is like to *be* black)[17] prison narratives also reveal the effects of apartheid structures and mythology. The double load of black women is most graphically revealed in Makhoere's prison memoir, as her father was a policeman and actually led the police to her hiding-place. Family and state both become authoritarian betrayers and Makhoere's narrative reflects this in its scenes of verbal and physical violence, and in the long act of resistance that her prison career was at every level of prison life. She had also been a single teenage parent before her sentence and imprisonment. As a result the collectivity she invokes is that of militant sisterhood completely outside the system and the country: armed resistance. She admires militarized women both for their abandonment of feminine stereotypes and their military power to destroy their enemies. Inside the prison she seeks to politicize and bind groups in resistance, and celebrates every minor victory.

Bessie Head's prison story, "The Collector of Treasures", set in independent Botswana, shows a similar movement from anger at unbearable degrees of subjection to male domination through an act of violence (Dikeledi murders her husband by castration) to the prison where she finds the "treasure" of other women's affection.[18] Dikeledi's crime is a common-law offence which Head links with the politically inspired breakdown of male integrity and family life over the time spans of traditional tribal life, colonialism and migrant labour, and independence.[19] She points out that in all three eras in Botswana, women have been regarded as an inferior form of life. Dikeledi, however, also has special traditional female skills: she can knit and thatch well. She is an image of the storyteller's interweaving and an instance of the way those creative skills are distorted and rechannelled into violence by intolerable levels of humiliation. This is a post-colonial society where the burdens on women have intensified, not eased. Post-colonial does not necessarily mean post-feminist. It is a comment on this society that the only freedom for Dikeledi is found in prison.

South African novelist Miriam Tlali's account of a "detour into detention" is also very angry, outraged at every level by the violence done to her and others on the occasion of a group arrest just before Steve Biko's funeral.[20] The violation is experienced intensely and subjectively at all levels, as a black woman, as a mother, as an oppressed citizen. She draws on metaphors of motherhood as a key image when she sees a young girl being molested by a policeman:

> My God! Whose daughter was it, I asked myself. It could have been my very own, I thought, all the nerves of my abdomen curling up into a painful knot. I could not bear the sight. The poor girl turned her eyes to me, and in them was a look no mother could mistake. It was a challenge, an appeal from a child, a female, to its mother.[21]

Here the family and the oppressed black "nation" are experienced as one: as the trade union slogan puts it: "an injury to one is an injury to all." Even while recording the breakdown of family life, then, both Makhoere and Tlali draw on metaphors of family bonding as the deepest connections they know. Political violence summons up the need for care and protection, which family love is meant to guarantee even if it has not been actively experienced. There is no self-conscious fictional manipulation or criticism of the family itself, and no suggestion that certain power structures or abuses may be replicated within the family, even in the case of Makhoere, who sees her father as trapped within his collaborative role, which indeed he is.

The two "white" prison narratives I wish to consider, those of Ruth First and Nadine Gordimer, are both by middle-class intellectuals who wish to record the experience of imprisonment in South Africa, though one is a memoir and the other a novel. Both writers reveal the difficulty of being the "half-colonized", i.e. women who may have experienced forms of domination within a patriarchal culture but whose position of power over a black majority is guaranteed by that same culture. Ruth First was the only woman associate of the Rivonia group, and was detained in 1963 under the Ninety-day no-trial law. The police pointed out to her that she occupied a "special" place because she was a woman:

> We know all about that meeting at Rivonia. It was a meeting of picked people from all over the country. Mandela was there, and Sisulu. The pick of the bunch. You're the only woman there... and you try to pretend that you know nothing of what happened, that you can't remember, that nothing happened worth knowing. We know all about you... You can count your lucky stars that we still have respect for women in our country. You could have been charged in the Rivonia case. But we didn't want a woman in that case. We still have some feeling for women.[22]

First's most obvious solidarity is with a particular class, a Johannesburg Jewish intelligentsia committed to the Communist Party, often lawyers with a strong sense of justice and its abuses in the country, the class, in fact whose inner predicaments Nadine Gordimer explores in her fiction (she may well have been drawing partly on her knowledge of the First/ Slovo family in her novel *Burger's Daughter*). First reveals her contempt for the Afrikaans prison wardresses on the grounds of their ignorance, their blind political affiliations, and their vulgarity (she calls them, after Snow White's seven dwarves: "Shrill", "Raucous" and "Pained)". Makhoere's resistance towards her wardresses, on the other hand, is often physical, though she also despises their stupidity, and her physical fights with them reflect their far greater readiness to use physical violence on her than they would on a white woman. First shows no solidarity with common-law prisoners, but writes of them with a mixture of amusement and social worker's sympathy.[23]

First's allegiance is to a political group and their programme, broadly the Freedom Charter and the multi-racial politics of the original ANC cell. This is revealed in her narrative structure: she constantly broadens the scope of her own prison memoir by recounting other prison lives, whether parallel to her own or not, in italicized sections within her narrative, the stories of Dennis Brutus, Dennis Goldberg, and Looksmart Ngudle. These italicized sections offer historical information, court proceedings, dramatic escapes, political events, interrogations and torture. They form extensions of her own experience, dramatize the noises she hears outside (the gunshot she hears at Brutus's arrest, for instance), and recount information she only had access to after her release. These stories add colour and drama to the monotony of her 117 days and add the stories of other lives and selves unlike her own, black experience of torture, male parallels to female experience. They offer a sense of a larger commitment, of continuity and repetition. They reveal both her desire to be more inclusive and representative than she feels she is, and her skills as a journalist and writer. Her story becomes a complex interwoven narrative, creating solidarity by intellectual and artistic means, not as a visceral response drawing on vivid emotive metaphors (as Tlali does). She is consciously broadening the scope of a white middle-class woman's experience by including other lives, other fates.

First reveals no special solidarity with women as such, and she deliberately keeps her children's lives in the background; she makes a conscious decision not to think of them too much. Her narrative is like her own lifelong political commitment: it takes the same shape. She strives for detachment from her own experience and suffering, to see them in their historical perspective. She offers her own biographical data last, as if to suggest her own minor role, to show that she does not see herself as central or representative in the political struggle. These are the signs of her own intellectual courage, and they did not prevent her from receiving the same punishment, eventually, as other more representative political prisoners.

First, then, shared the fate of the oppressed people with whom she sympathized and identified, but her narrative shows that the act of writing in her case becomes a self-conscious bridge between herself and a dispossessed majority. She is not a feminist, but she reveals the courage of independent thought and action which have made her an inspiration to later women in the political struggle. The "special place" the police told her she occupied is riddled with the ambiguities of special treatment: ironically, had they not given her the special treatment meted out to a woman, she might have been kept alive by the same incarceration as the rest of the Rivonia group, later delivered after many years in the belly of the whale. Her fate is almost a metaphor for the penalties incurred in that "special place" reserved for women by the respect of men. Respect is no substitute for equality and justice.

Nadine Gordimer is not a declared feminist either, but her fiction keeps exploring the psychic and physical manoeuvring space open to a half-colonized white woman in South Africa. A short story, "The Smell of Death and Flowers", suggests that a young white girl has to confront her own sexuality and perhaps break the patriarchal taboos of the white tribe before she can be liberated into the real world of political choices and political action.[24] *Burger's Daughter*, as the title indicates, sets up complex metaphoric transferences between family and state, daughterhood and citizenship, prison and liberation. The daughter of the title, Rosa Burger, seeks to find herself in the untrammelled pleasures of European culture, climate and art. Seeking to flee both a politicized family and the penalties they have incurred (her parents have both been political prisoners; her father dies in prison) she turns to the sunny pleasures of the Riviera and the company of her father's former mistress, Katya, but a love affair with an older man and a quarrel with a young black brother in exile send her home again, more experienced both in love and in grief and able to take on new commitments after these semi-incestuous experiences have freed her from the compulsions of the nuclear family. Rosa Burger arrives at a point where she takes her father's place in prison: the watermark of light on the prison wall repeats an earlier watermark she used to notice in her father's house.[25] Some critics have read this ending as a non-feminist capitulation, but Rosa is imprisoned while working with young black children, a "feminine" and nurturing occupation which leads her into her new place, a freely chosen "prison" in which she accepts the meaning of daughterhood. The final space she occupies, where friends visit and joke about the family, is not compelled: her experiences have taught her that law, in the family, might not be dissociated from love and that recognition unlocks her ability to challenge unjust laws in the state. She is able to repeat her father's commitment without feeling forced to do so by her position as his daughter. Both daughterhood and citizenship become choices, not submissions to authority.

An earlier experience in the novel, the death of a hobo in a city park which Rosa witnesses without comprehending until she reads about it in the newspaper[26] is a trigger for an understanding of mortality outside prisons, outside the apartheid system, for which there is no blame and no exoneration. Her family have taught her that everything would change once political change was effected, after the revolution. But here she confronts the "mystery itself" of absolute limitation, and absolute freedom:

> Nothing that had served to make us sure of what we were doing and why had anything to do with what was happening one lunchtime while I was in the square. I was left with that. It had been left out. Justice, equality, the brotherhood of man, human dignity – but it will still be there, I looked away everywhere from the bench and saw it still, when – at last – I had seen it once.[27]

Family life seems to supply us with metaphors for a humiliating dependency as well as a liberating acceptance of self: prison and prison literature seem to do the same. They remind us that boundaries exist and that individual identity, whether personal or national, is always fought for and maintained at a price. Individual rights, like the rights of peoples, need to be constantly re-asserted in a process of historical struggle. Independence, these writers seem to tell us, is found in the testing of limits. Our identities are corporeal, and we all speak from specific places and cultures which shape our responses, to life as well as literature. If we are to be emancipated, Gordimer's novel suggests, the microcosm of the family, which relies on the relationship between love and law, could provide a way into a more equitable model of the state. Shakespeare's Portia, in *The Merchant of Venice*, provides a similar insight into the paradoxical liberation of female identity; hemmed in by her father's prohibition in the ritual of the three caskets, she discovers that this paternal injunction has been constructed, like a magic gate, to let in the one suitor who is worthy of her and, for that reason, the one suitor she is capable of loving.

There is no post-feminism in the sense of moving beyond struggle, but the liberation the individual finds in the acceptance of personal responsibility, for which I've been using the model of liberated daughterhood, is the only guarantee we have that our post-colonial or post-apartheid worlds will be an improvement on the old world of dominance and slavery. Our surest path into a shared trans-national human condition lies in the defence of specific rights, and specific freedoms.

Notes

1. Ashcroft *Empire* 36.

2. Ibid 37.

3. Tiffin "Post-Colonialism".

4. Foucault *Discipline.*

5. Ngugi *Detained* xi.

6. Ibid 4.

7. Ashcroft *Empire* 26.

8. Delaney 35.

9. Makhoere 28.

10. Ngugi *Detained* 43.

11. First *Days* 128.

12. Harlow 128

13. Ibid 28.

14. Makhoere 103.

15. Moss 232.

16. MacKenzie 61.

17. Lewin 14.

18. Head *Collector* 87-103.

19. Ibid 91-92.

20. Tlali *Mihloti* 2-41.

21. Ibid 11.

22. First *117 Days* 120.

23. Ibid 31.

24. Gordimer *Selected* 122-144.

25. Gordimer *Burger's* 361.

26. Ibid 74-76.

27. Ibid 80.

Radical Transformations: Emergent Women's Voices in South Africa

Black South African women's writing demonstrates features of continuity and discontinuity with post-colonial women's literatures in other "Commonwealth" countries. One specific historical difference stems from the double colonization of the original indigenous population, first by the Dutch (Afrikaner/Boer), ideologically and militarily since 1652, and intermittently by the English, who withdrew in stages marked by the formation of union in 1910, the accession of the National Party in 1948, and the foundation of the Republic in 1961. Whereas externally colonized countries such as Australia and Canada have been decolonizing only in terms of English cultural hegemony and the centrist culture of British literary traditions, black South Africans have needed a double decolonization in terms of English cultural hegemony, and in terms of Afrikaner Nationalist rule since 1948. A brutal internal oppression has been in place since 1948, and has been subjected to refinements leading up to the imposition of emergency rule since June 1986.[1] Black South African writing is thus still properly a resistance literature, not a "post-colonial" one, and the resistance is still primarily against "white power;" not much distinction is drawn between English speakers and Afrikaners.[2]

Paradoxically, the tightening of internal, domestic "colonialism" by the Nationalist government, the intensifying of cultural hegemony (the attempt to enforce Afrikaans as a language of instruction in Black schools in 1976 which erupted in wide-scale violent protest) has encouraged a sense of the attractions of English as a political tool, a bridge to the West, a universal medium of communication, and a possible bearer of African culture.[3] Thus one factor discouraging a widespread commitment to vernacular languages has been the enforced isolation created by apartheid policy. The counter-discourse of resistance, protest, and cultural affirmation in South Africa has generally not included an insistence on linguistic decolonization.[4]

However, other ideological factors involved in the emergence of a broad, non-racial democratic front in the eighties, such as the felt need to communicate with a mass audience of peasants and workers, have created a renewed emphasis on African language communication, orature, and performance culture.

Much of black South African women's writing in the eighties is situated within this broader political context: one in which a commitment to an African destiny[5] through cultural pride and affirmation exists alongside non-racial principles and collaboration based on the Freedom Charter and the spirit of the ANC. Writers are renamed "cultural workers;" they may write in English or an African language; they draw on a range of African and European genres (story, poem, script, dialogue, praise-poem, interview); they point directly to past and present abuses of power in the polity or the workplace, and favour the direct impact of oral delivery and the "spontaneity" of poetry.[6] This orature and fugitive literature is collective in spirit, dedicated to socio-political ends, and often explicitly divorced from literary evaluation and aesthetic norms, though standards of writing and language skills are sometimes debated.[7] In this it is part of a traditional overweighting of political and socio-economic elements in South African literature, of message as against medium (Cornwell). In emphasizing factors other than literary excellence, it joins recent pleas within Commonwealth criticism for description and socio-political context rather than the instant literary judgment or dismissal which may be based on Eurocentric or colonial norms.[8] This broad non-racial alliance of writers exists alongside a remaining Black Consciousness ideology which crystallized more dramatically around 1976, with the crisis in schools and townships, and alongside a more individualist emphasis within an older generation of writers: Sipho Sepamla, Es'kia Mphahlele, and Miriam Tlali,[9] The collective spirit and the organization of literary statement around slogans, external apartheid symbols and typification rather than an attention to the individual inner life and aesthetic standards have also been critically examined.

How, then, does black women's writing situate itself in relation to this broader pattern of black resistance, evolving from Black Consciousness to non-racial cultural construction ("One Nation-One Culture"), though united by a strong didacticism and a tension between individual and collective utterance? I propose to look at the relationship between forms of oppression and subjective response in a spectrum of these writings by black women writers.[10] One broad continuity between these writings, and between them and other post-colonial women's writing, lies in the actual process of self announcement, the breaking of the silence of a very marginalized group: "women fighting their way out of silence to project more authentic images of how women feel and what they do," and mixing genre codes in doing so.[11]

Black South African women's writing also needs to be seen against the backdrop of African feminism, which has always been reluctant to dissociate itself from the whole community's broader cultural and political struggle for basic rights and human recognition.[12] "A woman's place is in the struggle," but, increasingly, black South African women have noticed that gender oppression can be ignored within progressive political organizations, and have established separate women's forums within them. Women's writing and orature within COSAW and COSATU reflects this complex affiliation to "Africanness" and "struggle;" the dominant voice can be protest against an oppressive racism ("I am African") or against class exploitation (unsafe working conditions) or against gender oppression (the pain of womanhood).[13] "Motherhood" becomes an image in which forms of protest fuse ("the child's mother always grabs the sharp end of the knife"), just as the domestic worker becomes the locus of triple oppression, the slavery at the base of the capitalist order and of the evolution of the South African state.[14] In this body of literature, the slave and the mother seem to hold a dialogue with each other, they are aspects of the same person.

But while black women's writing explicitly declares its positive aims of self-affirmation and collective purpose, dedicating itself to a post-apartheid future, and calling up heroic female figures from the history of resistance to strengthen resolve, it is undermined from within by the negative images and emotions inculcated by the "cultural bomb" of colonial domination and white racism, as well as the lack of confidence induced by the traditional inferior status of African women. As Ngugi argues, the most important area of colonial domination "was the mental universe of the colonized, the control, through culture, of how people perceived themselves and their relationship to the world."[15] What is often projected emotionally by the writers in *Women in South Africa: From the Heart*, an anthology of mainly first publications by women, is a deep sense of helplessness, grief, and an inchoate anger which moves among different objects, focusing now on an abusive father, now on a neglectful husband, now on the callousness of a white madam, a corrupt black collaborator, a sexually abusive employer or policeman. The protagonist of one story reflects:

> She could not define her feelings in any clearer terms, All she felt was a smouldering centre burning away inside her. She knew it involved her life, her sense of self and womanhood.[16]

Helplessness and grief lead to the repeated motif of the "blues"- the blues of washerwoman or mother-or to the violence which often effects the closure of plot: a knife goes into a policeman "full tilt," or a young girl kills her brutal father and hears him roar like a "dying lion".[17] The other mood is one of self-righteous generosity towards enemies or oppressors, inside and outside the family. Healing can be provided by the solidarity of other women, or the bonds of the family which tighten against white racists.[18]

The writing in *Women in South Africa* does not reveal a high degree of historical or political awareness: it reflects the intense emotions of women under apartheid, patriarchal power, class exploitation and gender discrimination. Pressures of the extended family, of incessant childbearing, of indifferent employers in home or workplace, sheer overwork combined with the personal impact of external political events or crises, provide the themes and plots of stories, scripts and poems. There is a strong didactic element, especially directed at other women who may need information: on contraception, or the pitfalls of non-recognition or abuse at the workplace ("we lift as we climb"). As Ndebele has remarked of the level of non-awareness induced by the numbing effects of apartheid in "Bantu education":

> it is largely untouched by much of the discourse of western philosophy... buzz words and expressions such as "human rights," "free enterprise," "human dignity," self-determination and other standardized

political vocabulary, have not been absorbed to the extent that they would figure prominently in the people's subjective experience of political language.[19]

The language of these women writers in *Women in South Africa* is simple and subjective; autobiography and fiction are almost indistinguishable: the authority claimed is "the authority of experience."[20] Against their invisibility in the South African state and awareness they assert, by writing or performance, that "a presence has been maintained." The "mere act of writing, of finding time, let alone space to do so, is in itself an act of monumental significance."[21] The act of self-assertion is extended in the brief CV and the photograph which prefaces each contribution, affirming individual identity. In the act of writing and publication, the subjective self is given a coherence not experienced in daily life under apartheid. Charles T. Davis has argued that in the complex relation of the "Black rhetorical self" to culture the "trope of absence" (the invisible *woman*) leads to the trope of *presence*.[22] This is evident everywhere in the texts, production and format of black South African women's writing. The accession to literacy is an important moment in this process, and should be recognised alongside the political pressure toward orature.[23]

The language of *Women in South Africa*, and the language of these works generally, is a polite, genteel English, lacking the raciness or dialectal strength found in the work of comparable male "township" writing, and reflecting the extent to which Christianity and social decorum have formed a buffer for women exposed to the instability and dislocations of apartheid, migrant labour, and family breakdown.[24] In Miriam Tlali's writing there is a much more conscious deployment of African phrases, proverbs and folktales, and she draws more consciously on the oral tradition to oppose both colonial imposition and the fragmentation of African support systems, though she will use the occasional quotation from Western literature when it suits her purpose.[25] She adapts genre in the same way, calling a description of detention "New Journalism" and including a visit to a "homeland holiday resort" under "travelogues".[26] Such manipulations of Western genres set up their own ironies. She adapts the more impersonal Western interview to the township situation of dialogue, laughter and interruptions, making it resemble a playscript. She sharply registers the physical discomforts, banalities and grossness of a second-class citizen's life, and the daily humiliations of black women's life inside and outside marriage. Her stories draw on the popular modes of melodrama, pathos, and romance, but always to make a political point: the lovers on Mt Qoqolosi will soon be separated by migrant labour; the couple in "Point of No Return" are parting because of the husband's political commitment, which is historically described and motivated in an internal narrative by him to her. Her stories often dramatize the process of politicization itself or are intended to raise the consciousness of her audience to feminist and social issues.[27] Her women share the ruses and strategies of a vulnerable group in a dangerous society, and establish support systems and emotional solidarity. The stories are themselves part of this communication and support system. Characters, rendered passionately from the inside, are shown grappling with a myriad petty and large abuses of power and bureaucracy,

Tlali's writing shows white South African racists as perceived by blacks, bent on maximum profits and on a daily denial of fellow feeling. Her female solidarity is with other black women only and thus the stories, even in their women's protest, remain within the parameters of Black Consciousness.

Within those parameters, though, her development has been towards a firmer articulation of women's oppression. The last story in her new collection deals with the problem of marital infidelity, a conniving wife and the "feminist" issues arising, but does so in a spirit of human consideration and community ethics rather than with the Western feminist emphasis on individual female rights or equality. Again, African humanism is a shaping force, modifying Western feminist ideology. Tlali's Soweto train story ("Fud-u-u-a!") also shows women sharing private but representative humiliations and thus adds a female perspective to the topos of the township train story, as previously established by male writers.[28] Tlali's strength lies in the angry rendering of everyday social injustice as lived by credible individuals forced into decisions and commitments by their outrage at the normality and continuity of injustice.[29] Her stories document sexual and racial harassment and show how deeply intertwined they are in South Africa. At the same time, the texture of her prose, and the Africanization of Western genres and ideologies, affirm an African identity, and

118

an ability to remould Western language and forms to her own needs.

A younger generation of women, working in the more recent non-racial spirit, do sometimes extend their sense of female oppression to include white women, though this kind of sisterhood has usually only been expressed in the other direction.[30] In the kind of poem recently written by Gcina Mhlope, "We are at War", all women become "Mother Africa's loved daughters" and the sense of female courage levers apart the racial barriers of South African society:

We are at War

Women of my country
Young and old
Black and white
We are at War
The winds are blowing
against us
We are at war
But do not despair
We are the winning type
Let us fight on
Forward ever
Backward never

Women of my country
Mothers and daughters
Workers and wives
We are at war
customs are set
against us
Religions are set
against us
But do not despair
We are bound to win
Let us fight on
Forward ever
Backward never

Women of my country
Mother Africa's loved daughters
Black and white
we are at war
Forces of exploitation
degrade mother Africa

as well as us, her daughters
Her motherly smile is ridiculed
She has seen her children sold
Her chains of slavery are centuries old
There is not time for us to cry now

She has cried rivers of tears
What is it that flows down River Nile
if not her tears
What is it that flows down River Congo
if not her tears
What is it that flows down River Zambezi
if not her tears
What is it that flows down River Limpopo
if not her tears
What is it that flows down River Thukela
if not her tears
and what is it then, that flows down River Kei
if not Mother Africa's tears
Women of Egypt and Libya
Drink her tears from River Nile
You will gain courage and bravery
Women of Congo and Liberia
Drink her tears from River Congo
You will shed inferiority
Women of Zambia and Zimbabwe
Drink her tears from River Zambezi
You will gain understanding
Women of South and West Africa
Drink her tears from River Limpopo
You shall see liberation
We are chained women of Africa
We are bound to win
Let us fight on
Forward ever
Backward never.[31]

In this poem the transhistorical fact of female pain, biologically rooted, fuses with the historical condition of slavery. Female suffering across colour lines and countries becomes a new rhetorical bridgehead against apartheid and nationalism.[32]

The cultural transformation which is achieved in black women's writing in the eighties is the transformation of the black woman as object, interpreted only in the colonial or liberal gaze, and previously obscured by guilt or projection, and sheer ignorance, into a speaking subject. The social details of black women's lives, as given externally in the short stories of Nadine Gordimer, or the mediating narration of Elsa Joubert, are registered from the inside, by the woman who sometimes lives in the maid's room, or receives the madam's cast-off clothing.[33] Not only does she speak for herself, eluding the bad faith of white spokeswomanship, she also speaks as representative of a community of women, some of whom are illiterate.[34] The quality of the writing is, for the moment, irrelevant. A whole continent of previously repressed or invisible consciousness comes to light for the first time. The dimensions of such grief and anger, once revealed, demand a response, and must be confronted. In speaking to a largely black audience and articulating her grievances, the black woman writer also addresses a white constituency which has always preferred her invisibility and silence. The shift in white consciousness which such writing can cause makes a contribution to a rapidly evolving social formation. The African struggle for liberation, says Ngugi, "is an ever-increasing struggle to seize back their creative initiative in history through a real control of all the means of communal self-definition in time and space."[35] This is doubly true for African women, who have always been defined by others, whites and men.

Black South African women's writing, in grappling with specific socio-political realities, and releasing the emotional pressures they bring about, reveals a very different imaginative configuration to that of a Nadine Gordimer, whose novel, *A Sport of Nature*, has sought to embody a vision of a possible post-colonial, post-apartheid woman. Gordimer's heroine is the final fantasy of white female colonial vision, seeking vitality and power in sexual alliance with black male revolutionary leaders. For the black women writers discussed here, liberation is a practical daily struggle connected with a wider national struggle. It keeps defining the ground of possible collaboration against a necessary separatism, both as blacks and women.[36] Other women are seen as resources of information and assistance, not sexual rivals in the traditional pursuit of power over men, who in turn confer political power. Writing itself becomes, in their hands, only one form of action to bring about the radical transformation of South African society. It is the imaginative response to historical fact and historical pain which transforms both individuals and societies. Literature and orature vividly dramatize historical conditions and thus these writers reach out to the national imagination. Urgent priorities shape their vision and emphasis, and should perhaps also shape the critical practice which receives them.

"Women's day today is freedom day tomorrow."

Notes

I should like to thank Boitumelo Mofokeng for the substantial informal discussion concerning recent writing and ideology on which this paper draws (Mofokeng); also Es'kia Mphahlele for commentary and useful discussion, and Cecily Lockett for suggestions and a preliminary reading of the paper.

1. Adam *Modernizing.*

2. Point made by Boitumelo (Tume) Mofokeng and in discussion with Es'kia Mphahlele. See also JanMohammed: "In the colonial situation the function of class is replaced by race" (7).

3. For a full discussion of the uses of English by black South Africans, and its ideological implications, see Mphahlele, who argues that English "provides a Pan-African forum" for the black South African writer, though indigenous languages will always be the bearer of immediate culture. English unifies ethnic groups and has always been the vehicle of African nationalism (discussion, 21 August 1989). See also Ndebele (1987), who argues against the "benevolent containment" implied in the identification of the English language with education, and suggests that "The Commonwealth... is an alliance of historically captive users of English. It is cultural practice which needs to be altered: "indigenous languages can be a refuge away from the manipulative impersonality associated with corporate English language acquisition."

4. Ngugi *Decolonizing.*

5. "Most African writers write out of an African experience and of commitment to an African destiny" (Achebe 50).

6. Boitumelo Mofokeng in *Buang Basadi.*

7. *Buang* 17.

8. Tiffin "Commonwealth".

9. Conversation with Sipho Sepamla, August 1989. Es'kia Mphahlele emphasizes that Black Consciousness was and is not exclusivist; it is "the intensified moment of self-pride and self-reliance;" it expresses the inner self and consciousness, He also stresses the continuity of Black Consciousness from the nineteenth century and Edward Blyden's concept of the African personality, developed in Liberia (Discussion, 21 August 1989).

10. I have concentrated on *Women in South Africa. From the Heart – An Anthology,* writing collected in *Buang Basadi,* and in *Black Mamba Rising: South African Worker Poets in Struggle,* Miriam Tlali's *Mihloti* and *Footprints in the Quag.* Some of the writers concerned first published in *Staffrider* magazine. Ellen Kuzwayo's autobiography, *Call Me Woman,* and Zinzi Mandela's *Black as I Am* are other reference points.

11. Howells 5.

12. See Frene Ginwala, "ANC Women: Their Strength in the Struggle," and also Katherine Frank, who argues that "African society... places the values of the group

over those of the individual with the result that the notion of the African feminist almost seems a contradiction in terms" (45).

13. See, for instance, "When I was born…" and "A Mother's Cry" by Boitumelo Mofokeng in *Women in South Africa: From the Heart*, pp. 92, 94, and "I, The Unemployed" by Nise Malange in *Black Mamba Rising: South African Worker Poets in Struggle*.

14. "The contemporary economic exploitation of nonwhites in South Africa has its ultimate roots in slavery and indentured servitude" (JanMohamed *Manichean Aesthetics* 82). Emergent black women's writing in South Africa shows some affinity with American slave narratives which told stories of life under the yoke to mobilize support for the anti-slavery movement, and in which the lust of the white master often figured: see Mpine Qakisa's "Storm on the Mine Dumps" (*WiSA* 154-60). The power of such narratives comes from the vivid impression of life under bondage, Charles T. Davis argues. It is significant that the imagination of the first white woman novelist, Olive Schreiner, should also have been fired by the figure of the slave, and reveals similar characteristics (see, for instance, the short story, "Dream Life and Real Life"). Schreiner's key modes, severe victimization or aloof forgiveness and sacrifice for wrongs, are also repeated in the writing under consideration.

15. Ngugi *Decolonizing* 16.

16. *Women* 89.

17. *Women* 39, 50.

18. See the ending of Dinah Lefakane's "Old Man River" (*WiSA* 71), and Bessie Head's "The Collector of Treasures" (in the volume of that name) in which the castration of a brutal husband is followed by the finding of the "treasure," the love of other women.

19. Ndebele "English" 7.

20. Diamond.

21. Diamond 7.

22. Davis xviii, xxi.

23. See Kuzwayo's announcement, "I am the author of this book" (55).

24. The African Independent Churches have a following of 7 million, of which 70% are women, who find in these churches a source of solidarity, support and spiritual endurance for suffering.

25. See, for instance, Tlali's *Mihloti* (106), where a Victorian quotation on angling is followed by the African vernacular word for dawn, "mafube".

26. Tlali *Mihloti* 96-109.

27. "Feminist" is a Western term used only once in *Women in South Africa: From the Heart*; black women seldom use it to define themselves (point made in discussion, Linda Gilfillan, AUETSA conference, July 1989).

28. See Bereng Setuke's "Dumani" and Mango Tshabangu's "Thoughts in a Train" in *Forced Landing*.

29. Ndebele cites her strengths in "Turkish Tales," and Gareth Cornwell points to her "faction" and its enduring strengths.

30. See, for instance, Ingrid de Kok's poem, "Small Passing" in *Familiar Ground.*

31. Brown 159-160.

32. The idea of biological essentialism has become a heresy in feminist theory, but the ability to bear children and the effects of this biological difference seem to be crucial in this writing. Tlali writes: "The women were smiling, watching and giving each other all the moral support women in need of help ought to give each other. "We're all alike, we're women. We need each other when things are difficult because we have given birth to children. Wherever one goes one hears women say, "we have to feed our children, haven't we?" ("Fud-u-u-a!," *Footprints in the Quag*, p. 30). There is a lot of foster-mothering in the situations of political distress described by Tlali, as in "Detour into Detention" (*Mihloti* 2-41) in which Tlali protects one young girl and sees another teenage girl appeal to her while she is beaten. Motherhood is extended into a metaphor for protection and care; it is constructed as a site of intense vulnerability and intense courage.

33. See, for instance, "Ah, Woe Is Me," and "Happy Event" in Gordimer's *Selected Stories*, and Elsa Joubert's *The Long Journey of Poppie Nongena.*

34. Discussion with Tume Mofokeng. Poems by domestic workers also feature in *Buang Basadi.*

35. Ngugi *Decolonizing* 4.

36. Es'kia Mphahlele says of recent black women's writing that it is "straining towards self-definition; the mould has not yet set; different voices are coming in." This "looking for a place" in the literature is an expression of the African woman's looking for a place in the wider society, her social instability. (Discussion, 21 August 1989.)

Women's Writing:
What's New in South Africa (1993)

It is only recently that a sufficient spectrum of writing by white and black women in South Africa has emerged that can flesh out the complex positions and lived experience of all women in South Africa. This spectrum has been apparent in the appearance of anthologies of women's writing, journals and perhaps most significantly, the publication of a whole new generation of women's voices forged in the recent struggles around gender and race. These South African women have argued that gender and racial oppression go together and should be contested simultaneously. Recent writings testify to many subtle forms of silencing, an internalizing of male norms, a depiction of conventional colonial marriage as a prison (a key early text here was Doris Lessing's *The Grass is Singing*) as well as testimony to the brutal control of black women by traditional African patriarchy and arranged marriages. Dramatist and popular story teller Gcina Mhlope's story, "Nokulunga's Wedding" reveals the abuses inherent in traditional African power structures. Other stories and sketches represent the predicaments of contemporary African women resulting from a double standard of sexual morality, harassment and assault on overcrowded township trains, the breakdown of traditional extended family support, and the impact on the family of decades of violent struggle.

It has been said that patriarchy was re-invented in the colonies. The complex interweavings of racial and gender oppression in South Africa, despite the class and economic differences which separate white from black women, have made women a marginal group both in the traditional power structures of British imperialism and

Afrikaner nationalism and in the current restructuring of the South African polity. Historian Jeff Guy has argued that the appropriation and control of women's productive and reproductive capacity by men was the central dynamic of pre-capitalist farming society in Southern Africa. Nevertheless, women had some autonomy and control of the agricultural process.

In the uneven transition to capitalist relations of production new forms of oppression emerged and the assumption of male authority over women was reinforced. Western norms circumscribed the position of black women, migrant labour created intense pressure on the African family, and missionary interventions weakened the older family support systems. Colonial authorities entrenched customary law in a way which exacerbated the difficulties of African women: the outer form of the indigenous sex-gender system was preserved while its inner logic was destroyed. Settler native policy evolved in the context of a voracious demand for cheap black labour and the reserve system which underwrote this male black labour system in turn created new constraints on the freedom of black women. Black women, as Writer Ellen Kuzwayo recently pointed out, were the last to reach the cities and attempt to tap into a swollen squatter population and dwindling opportunities. Prostitution, beer-brewing and domestic service were the poor choices available. Historian Philip Bonner has argued that the beer-brewers and prostitutes on the Rand could at least claim some autonomy for themselves in their flight from a shattered family system.

Thus modern South Africa has a racially-stratified sex-gender system in which South African women are discriminated against as blacks and as women. Some sociologists argue that this system turns white women into Southern-type managers of the estate's slave labour: certainly the fiction of a writer like Nobel Prize winner Nadine Gordimer has constantly testified to the interdependent but unequal prison of madam and maid in the South African household. Gordimer's main target has, however, always been the racially oppressive system of apartheid, so much so that she could dismiss the feminist protests of her forerunner, Olive Schreiner as an irrelevant side issue. Gordimer's 1987 novel, *A Sport of Nature,* was problematic for many feminists, but some younger readers feel it attempts to validate a discourse of the body which at least opposes the discourses of racial categorization.

A second major international figure, J. M. Coetzee, has also begun to give gender issues more space and attention. Coetzee's *Age of Iron* is a moving novel as letter from a dying mother (and a dying liberalism) to a daughter in North America. The letter is thrown across a cultural gap whose damaging effects are chronicled in the mother's story. The novel may also suggest that the loss of liberalism, and the long political struggle for a kind of justice in South Africa, with the sacrifices involved, may have resulted in a petrification of the heart for all concerned. The death of Coetzee's protagonist, Elizabeth Curren, may also mean the death of a compassionate nurturance which she also represents. Coetzee's constant attempts to engage with a female sensibility represent a continuing effort to broach the boundaries of gender. Another male writer who has attempted to give women's lives a central focus is Sipho Sepamla, whose *Third Generation* and *A Scattered Survival* show the details of women's resistance in township domestic life as a continuing and important aspect of South African life.

But the new situation of emergent women's voices has been stimulated by a number of other factors. Two major historical anthologies of women's writing appeared in 1990: Cecily Lockett's *Breaking the Silence* (poetry) and Annemarie van Niekerk's *Raising the Blinds* (short stories). These anthologies have made some kind of historical overview of the two genres possible, and they both treat writings by women of all races as a continuum, and acknowledge the role of women's writing as testimony and historical documentation. Nevertheless, the "minor" colonial voices drawn into their picture reveal how colonial women were often condemned to a realm of genteel triviality which was in itself imprisoning. Smaller but significant anthologies, such as *Women in South Africa: From the Heart*, have come from the black feminist publishing house, Seriti sa Sechaba in Johannesburg. For the first time women actually employed as domestic servants were writing or inventing their own stories and poems and finding a forum other than magazines like *Staffrider* in Johannesburg (in which women were always under-represented).

A few journals have also assisted in the process of making women visible. *Current Writing*, a strong critical journal from the University of Natal, has made gender issues a major concern. *The Southern African Review of Books*, now relocated from London to Cape Town, has begun to give gender issues more visibility and attention.

Another factor has been the continuing visibility of a few black women who have continued to write against the odds: Miriam Tlali and Ellen Kuzwayo. Miriam Tlali's first novel, *Muriel at Metropolitan* was an investigation of the daily treatment of a few black women in urban employment as second-class citizens. Tlali's recent writings, such as *Footprints in the Quag* have been more powerful interweavings of feminist anger and racial injustice. Ellen Kuzwayo's autobiography, *Call me Woman*, was an invaluable contribution to the documentation of African women's experience under Christianization, forced removals, unhappy marriage, urbanization, and politicization through a younger generation in the seventies. Women like Tlali and Kuzwayo in turn act as role models and stimulus to younger women who often lack the confidence to move into the cultural arena at all.

The cultural dimension of the recent political struggle has also played a role in that women within organizations such as COSAW (the Congress of South African Writers) have become more active and vociferous. Women praise poets drawing on a revitalized oral tradition, such as Nise Malange, have shown how women activists can harness language and public performance to trade union activity and general consciousness-raising.

The past decades of struggle have drawn women of different races together in new forms of cultural and political activity. Women writers continue to pose new questions that reveal the racially stratified sex-gender system that discriminates against South African women. One writer who reflects this world is Menan du Plessis, who has now written two novels exploring the mixed responses of young people in Cape Town, *A State of Fear* and *Longlive*. In her fiction the chequered idealism and personal loneliness of a younger generation growing up amidst constant violence are vividly portrayed. A changing political order has also meant more movement and reconciliation in the exiled community. Writer Lauretta Ngcobo, long exiled in London, has visited South Africa and produced a most triumphant and movingly elegiac novel about rural women's lives over many generations, *And They Didn't Die*. The circular structure of this novel suggests how many abuses of power remain, yet its main character embodies the continued expression of female resistance and strength. A younger writer, Zoe Wicomb, now teaching at the University of the Western Cape, has become a most articulate critic combining political acumen and literary insight. Her collection of short stories, *You Can't Get Lost in Cape Town*, is an extremely strong and well crafted vision of a "Coloured" childhood, of belonging and not belonging at many levels, to the country of one's birth. Her role as a critic and writer is very promising, as a new generation of voices is needed to forge a common culture where so much has been unquestioned for so long.

Much of the writing discussed here represents the continuing effects of many forms of dispossession, injustice and physical suffering in Southern Africa. Women's voices are now beginning to be more fully heard, and the complex interrelationship of racial and sexual oppression more fully documented. These writers form a crucial platform in the broad attempt to forge in South Africa a society and culture which will move out from under the shadow of a long and traumatic political tyranny and social fracture.

White Writing and Postcolonial Politics: Nadine Gordimer and J.M. Coetzee[1]

Nadine Gordimer and J. M. Coetzee are probably the two most widely known and internationally acclaimed white South African novelists, representing to world opinion, judging by the prizes they have received (the Nobel Prize for Literature to Gordimer in 1991 and the Jerusalem Prize to Coetzee in 1987 being only two of the most prestigious), voices of conscience and integrity within the developing and turbulent politics of South Africa. They have been involved also in continuing debates, conducted partly with each other by way of polemic and fiction, about the nature and significance of intellectual activity and novel writing during the changing decades of repression and resistance.[2] During the 1970s and 1980s a wide range of critical responses to their work, both South African and international (and partly determined by their respective locations in these two critical communities), arose in the process of the professionalization of Southern African critical debates and their progressive interlocking (and disagreement) with international theoretical models of postmodernism and postcolonialism.[3] Coetzee, in particular, seemed to be welcomed into an international critical community nourished by the same poststructuralist critics and linguists who appeared to form an intellectual substructure for his fiction or to provide appropriate tools for its analysis.[4] Here, at last, was a writer from South Africa on whom Lacanian analysis would not be wasted!

Gordimer's international reception has always been more clearly marked by the liberal humanism within which she seemed to locate herself, as the title of her volume of nonfiction, *The Essential Gesture*, indicates. She has spoken often, in her occasional nonfiction and public speeches, in terms of commitments, as a writer and a citizen, as if those commitments could be unproblematically made by a white intellectual and as if those two commitments existed on the same plane. Coetzee has been much more apt to speak in terms of privacy and freedom, especially the freedom not to be drawn into the intellectual compartments set up by contesting critical paradigms, whether South African or international, or, more simply, the power politics that have riven the South African scene and are refracted through academic life and criticism. Michael K, in his novel of the same name, is a not-too-distant relative of Coetzee's. Coetzee guards his privacy and the sources of his writing, despite his gradually more revealing interviews. In his interviews he has disclaimed the right to representative "committed" action or writing on behalf of anyone else in South Africa; the project of his fiction has been to explore the difficulties of any such gesture in South Africa or of any representation of otherness in any situation of power imbalance. Coetzee's fiction and criticism (his important nonfiction is collected with a telling sequence of interviews by David Attwell in *Doubling the Point*) conduct a running debate with history, as oppressive fact and as discourse, whereas Gordimer's argument (at least in terms of public discourse) has been conducted more literally and specifically in terms of her generation's political opposition to the South African state, the Nationalist Party, and apartheid.

This difference is partly generational: Gordimer was born in 1923 and has drawn her literary inspiration from Eastern European dissident thinkers (in a kind of intellectual acknowledgment of her otherwise elusive Jewish inheritance) and short-story writers such as Katherine Mansfield, though from the first the economic imbalances of the country and the specifically racial prejudices and fears of white South Africa formed the crux of her short stories. Coetzee, born in 1940, is a highly trained linguist whose specialized scholarship, including early studies in maths and computer science, has shaped both his syntax and his overriding interest in language as phenomenon, as an endless but problematic resource, as a cultural barrier and as a site where privilege and power are deeply inscribed, especially in South Africa. Beckett and Kafka have been returning and powerful presences in his fictions, shaping as they have our modern and postmodern awareness that alienation from self is an inseparable part of alienation from the simple exercise of political authority.[5] As is so often the case, an added twist occurs in the South African context, where there has been so much abuse of secrecy and surveillance. The South African scene was ripe for Coetzee's applications of the European absurdist fable to colonialism.

Attwell has pointed out that Coetzee is also a regional writer, and his "region," though more or less transmuted in each fictive terrain, is the Cape Province, including the Karoo, which he de-mythologizes, or re-mythologizes, in *In The Heart of the Country*. Gordimer was born in a small mining town on the Witwatersrand in the Transvaal, and her maturation accompanied the key clashes of Johannesburg liberalism and underground black struggle with the era of high apartheid and social engineering. As Stephen Clingman's book-length study charted, there has been no better guide to the social and inner life of decades of South African history (and to what Rowland Smith has called the "Johannesburg Genre") than Gordimer. The politicization of her heroines has represented a fictional refraction of her own.[6] Coetzee was born in the Cape Province and has made Cape Town his home: that windy island (peninsula) that seems so abstractly rendered in the literary territory of the opening pages of *Foe* is also recognizably Cape Town, and some of his most intimate effects involve the recognition of a known and loved landscape as well as the speech habits of the people who live there. He is not only regional; he presents a love of particular regions, in his character Michael K, for instance, as a humanizing though ineffectual bulwark against the dehumanization of racial politics. He knows (and loves) Afrikaans (and Dutch) in a way Gordimer does not. Both Coetzee and Gordimer have multiple, overlapping cultural and ethnic affiliations and disaffiliations that are nevertheless contained at another level by their South Africanness (and yet a South Africanness constituted, until now, by the experience of living within a white minority holding vast power and privilege over a disenfranchised black majority). Coetzee, who tends to be assimilated to a renegade Afrikaner modelled by Brink and Breytenbach, grew up in an English speaking home,[7] though some of his obsessive fictional mapping of early South African exploration in *Dusklands* must have its roots in a shared family tree, and even the intimacy of the hatred expressed by Elizabeth Curren in *Age of Iron* for the "boars" as patriarchal master race seems to stem from a disenchanted but knowledgeable descendant (in that sense the model of the renegade Afrikaner has some truth). *In The Heart of the Country* reveals that Coetzee knows about the Afrikaner master/servant relationship on South African farms, and the Oedipal tensions they carry, in a way that Gordimer does not, though her portrait of Johannesburg madam/male servant in *July's People*, and in many short stories, shows us what she knows inimitably well.

It is not, of course, the South Africanness of Coetzee and Gordimer that is at issue in many of the critical debates, but rather their whiteness and privilege within a political configuration that has so radically, until very recently, dispossessed and silenced a black majority. What right have they had to speak at all for those debarred from speech, if they have so spoken? And even if that very privileging has been their subject, as it has, has not their international fame and the thoroughness of their critical reception replicated their national situation internationally, ensconcing them ever more completely in the trappings of mediating liberal spokesmanship and cultural value? Are there not deserving and valid black (and "Coloured") viewpoints that are not being as widely articulated, circulated, and listened to? The current moment seems a good one in which to ask such questions and to recognize that there has been a certain self-confirming, circular relationship between white intellectual privilege in South Africa and an educated international public anxious to align itself with the voices of conscience emerging from a dark continent or a "police state." It is hard not to notice that all of the critics in the two volumes under review are white. And yet no one would wish to be without the literary testimony offered during decades of change by two such humane and intelligent writers from South Africa and by the increasingly sophisticated and humane critical responses they have called forth. They have themselves charted "from the inside," to echo Stephen Clingman's subtitle, the many sociopolitical shifts that have eventually precipitated a new order, have made the ambiguities of the white relationship to that process their subject, and, more so in the case of Coetzee, part of narrative process and a questioning of textuality itself. Moreover, international perceptions and images of South Africa have been created largely by Gordimer and Coetzee (as well as André Brink and Breyten Breytenbach, on a more sensationalist level) for an educated public, and the stimulus this might have given to economic and other sanctions (which undoubtedly played their part in bringing down the old order) was a political intervention hard to measure. Thus it seems important to ask how the by-now considerable oeuvres of these two white writers have affected and shaped national and international perceptions of a country so recently in the world spotlight when a major and long overdue shift in power occurred.

I

I want to argue, in a partial response to this question, that South Africa's intransigent position with regard to postcolonial theory, based on the little purchase that theory could have when the only postcolonial moment in South African history (until the second, more recent moment) coincided with the Nationalist imposition of apartheid,[8] has made it an illuminating case within critical debates over the political purchase of postmodernism and postcolonialism generally. The South African case might thus throw some light on current contestations of the political implications of "postmodernism," aesthetic practices, and the scope and relevance of a "postcolonial" critical practice in Canada. The two volumes under review are usefully read within this complex and continuing debate.

Bruce King's collection of essays on Gordimer's later fiction, conceived of as starting with her 1974 novel, *The Conservationist* (a neglected work to which Lars Engle's essay gives some fine, detailed attention), draws together much interesting work. King's own thesis is that Gordimer has basically remained within the genre of the *Bildungsroman*, while ringing many changes on that pattern as she tried to write "the new novel of Africa".[9]

Postmodern elements have not basically altered her conception of the relationship between the personal and the political, nor her location within critical realism. He makes useful links between Canadian Margaret Atwood's *Surfacing* and Gordimer's *July's People* as fictions that critique a return to the primitive as the basis for female renewal. John Cooke's essay draws on the few more direct autobiographical revelations Gordimer has made (of her mother's possessiveness and desire to maintain her daughter as an invalid) to discuss the movement in Gordimer's fiction between family structures and wider political commitments, seeing a condition of "lucky orphanhood" (that of Hillela in *A Sport of Nature*) as the precondition for action in the adult world.[10]

In a sense, Michael Wade's essay on Gordimer's evasive attitude to her Jewishness adds to this argument, in that an oppressive family romance is uncovered in more detail. Perhaps the sexual freedoms of Gordimer's heroines owe some of their provenance to the fantasies of irresponsibility nourished within this oppressive nuclear family; do women really slip in and out of relationships with so few scars, in the real world? It is partly Gordimer's failure to invest the main love affair of *Burger's Daughter* with real need (or a love beyond desire and narcissism) that lessens the value of Rosa's decision to return to South Africa. In *My Son's Story*, however, the political and familial repercussions of an (adulterous) love affair are exposed to a more searching analysis and carry more moral weight, even as the novel also investigates "the construction of a myth of authoring",[11] and thus ventures into terrain we associate more closely with Coetzee and the self-reflexiveness of the postmodernist project. Love affairs in Gordimer's fiction have usually been represented in terms of style (dare one say radical chic or *haute couture* sex?); this reaches its apotheosis in *A Sport of Nature* and creates some of this reader's unease with the alignment of Hillela's bodily freedom with a revolutionary utopian politics in Stephen Clingman's rich discussion of the novel in his essay in the collection. Are the connections between sensual pleasure and political commitment to countries that easy, or do they usually involve abrasive choices and losses? There is an important sense in which Gordimer's fiction trivializes the political (in terms of race as well as gender) by locating identity so overwhelmingly within the sensual.

In the real world (a term I will not italicize) the moment of liberation in South Africa was paved by human sacrifice, torture, ugliness, slow intellectual and cultural processes. The role played by white liberal women was minimal. In the unfolding world of Gordimer's fiction, however, the white woman's search for commitment, as Graham Huggan points out,[12] is central, and in *A Sport of Nature* her political role is finally central. Here lies a final form of self-deception: the sad and compromised realities of Winnie Mandela's situation on the day of Mandela's inauguration in Pretoria cast a retrospective light on the culminating scenes of *A Sport of Nature*, revealing them as an apotheosis of a white liberal woman's fantasy (among other things). However, Huggan is right to point out, too, that the dialectic between art and action in Gordimer's fiction is less resolved than ever in *A Sport of Nature*, and, like Rowland Smith,[13] he mentions the multiple ironies of her fictions as a key to her vision. Smith sees the "deadpan externality" of the ending of the novel as pointing to a detached scepticism about any human agents involved in political struggle.[14] In A Sport of Nature a white woman's drive towards a romantically represented union with black revolutionary heroism co-exists with an ambiguous presentation of the main protagonist, evident in the tone and narrative method. Perhaps this ambiguity represents that moment in South African oppositional consciousness when the rhetoric of struggle was making way for the more complex ironies of the real inauguration of a new order. Recent South African history itself has created a context within which black men who emerge like obsidian gods from the waves are decidedly suspect and within which we have to ask whether irony is enough (enough to counter this novelettish sexuality, and also ever a sufficient response to the pain of South African history). Daphne Read notes the stereotype of the sensually redemptive black figure in *Burger's Daughter*.[15] In comparison, Coetzee's schoolmaster Thabane in *Age of Iron* is a convincingly realistic figure. Can it be that postmodernists are more "realistic" than the realists?

Kathrin Wagner's conclusions to her discussion of landscape in Gordimer's fiction underline a related romantic response to nature.[16] She argues that the "hopeful naiveté" of the ending to *A Sport of Nature* demonstrates the extent to which Gordimer has remained in thrall to the residual stereotypes of colonialism, even as she inaugurates a postcolonial age.[17] This seems right: it is easier to see now that Gordimer's major fictions to date have coincided with a historical phase in South Africa within which whites were both liberal protestors and inescapably complicit. The liberal opposition in which Gordimer has been caught up forms one element in the ideological contestation that is staged for us in Coetzee's *Age of Iron*, more especially in the confrontation between Mrs Curren and Thabane. Gordimer speaks of waking up other white South Africans to their real political position and of wanting her fiction to be a consciousness-raising agent (as if her own position is not complicit). The extent to which she has achieved these results is hard to measure (though I would say I have been both irritated and moved, and thus changed, by each of her fictions). The record she has left, in being willing to follow her own fantasies into a warren "where many burrows lead off into the same darkness",[18] has exposed the workings of white fantasies as much as the historical phases of political struggle. She has always known this: "I have to offer you myself as my most closely observed specimen." What will become increasingly clear, as "blacks learn to talk and whites learn to listen,"[19] is that her fictional record is embedded in a racially stereotypic view of the world, one that coincided with the era of white control and privilege.[20] Gordimer's fiction has borne witness to many changes, but her perspective on those changes has not had the free space she has sometimes claimed for it. To put it Coetzee's way, she has not accepted as fully as he has that "the hand that holds the pen is only a conduit of the signifying process."[21] Furthermore, her commitment to the individual invented biography as the carrier of her critique, to what King calls the *Bildungsroman*, despite all the ways in which she has problematized her narrative presentation, has been both the strength of her psychosexual portrait of colonial womanhood and the boundary of its critical horizon. Gordimer's fiction demonstrates the strengths and limitations of a liberal humanist view that trusts the integrity of the politically serviceable subject and the eloquence of language as a carrier of moral vision founded on an opposition to apartheid politics. The trajectory of her fiction has shown a growing destabilization of the position of the author as she has responded to an aesthetic critique (with moral implications) embedded in the challenge of Coetzee's fictional enterprise.

II

Attwell's authoritative study of Coetzee's fiction was developed as a response to the failure of the left (more especially, of the terms of the critique set up by the South African left) to recognize Coetzee's achievement as a writer.[22] His view of Coetzee's "situational metafiction"[23] was put together from eclectic sources, drawing on developments within theory, interviews, his reading of Coetzee's major sources, and insights engendered in debates surrounding postcolonialism. His study is developmental, treating *Waiting for the Barbarians* as the pivotal text in Coetzee's progressive dismantling of cultural authority. He sees the early fiction as an attack on the rationalist, dominating self of colonialism and imperialism,[24] whereas the later fiction dramatizes more fully the limitations of white South African authorship. In a short, final discussion of *Age of Iron* Attwell sees Coetzee as having won through to a position of being more "explicit about South Africa and its obsessions".[25] He emphasizes the historicity of storytelling itself as he seeks to situate each novel against both contemporary political events and their related discourses.

If this approach seems a little cerebral and rigid in its patterning of the fiction, that is partly the result of Attwell's concise polemical approach. At times he seems to be in quest of a "transcendence" (his final phrase) for Coetzee's "engagement with history",[26] which Coetzee has ceased to claim for himself, if he ever claimed it. Nevertheless, his readings of the novels are rich and convincing, informed by local historical knowledge, researched sources, as well as contemporary theory. What Attwell does perhaps not address sufficiently are the ethical implications of the narrative "choices" Coetzee makes with each novel, and the sense one has of each novel as in part a return, with a difference, to a previous concern: with the position of colonial women, with the problem of colonial isolation, with the contamination of language, the need for wordlessness and love, the "language of the heart," "the resonance of the full human voice telling its stories",[27] which his early heroine, Magda, so desperately seeks and which Mrs Curren in *Age of Iron* has learned to speak because it is the language we all learn to speak in conditions of desolate extremity. Desolate extremities were what the 1980s were about in South Africa.

The connections between aesthetic practices and ethical issues in South Africa, as well as in Coetzee's work, are extremely well followed up in the set of essays collected by Michael Valdez Moses in a recent special issue of *The South Atlantic Quarterly*, a collection that also further modulates debates around postmodernism and postcolonialism and their articulation on the South African scene. Caroline

Rody, in an extension of Hutcheon's concept of the "complicitous critique"[28] from the postmodern to the postcolonial, argues that "in his tragicomic fables of the complicitous white soul, Coetzee bridges this divide (that between the postmodern and postcolonial), demonstrating the link between postmodern 'complicitous critique' and the nexus of race and power characteristic of postcolonial texts."[29] Philip Wood, in a complex interchange with Coetzee marked by extremely long questions and extremely short but clear (and modest) answers, writes that "this 'postmodern' turn is not the outcome of a turn from history... but rather the product of a head-on confrontation with an exceptionally problematic historical situation."[30] Furthermore, I would argue that it is precisely the postmodern turn that has facilitated a more fundamental critique of both a racially ordered society and colonialism generally by allowing a double critique, of power and of the cultural practices and forms of spokesmanship within which power is embedded. The self-reflexivity of Coetzee's writing, its interruptions of narrative process or reminders that it is a text (though not merely a text) we are reading, allows a simultaneous questioning of political power and textual authority to take place. We are constantly reminded that language itself is the instrument of a corrupting socialization that takes us away from true sources of power within ourselves while being the only means, or the fullest means, of communication with others. The South African case, and more especially the comparison between Gordimer and Coetzee suggested here, thus allows us to see that postmodernism as aesthetic practice allows a very full critique of an extreme colonialism.

Simon During, in his discussion of Nelson Mandela and Derrida, argues a similar case, that "Mandela reflects the west most powerfully in that he shows how the universals that have come to operate as signifiers of, and laws for, occidental identity undo the boundaries of their place of origin" and "speak with greatest force to those, like Mandela, from whom the West withholds the Law."[31] To put this another way, as Coetzee does, there are claims made by the suffering body, which takes a final right: "its power is undeniable."[32] This "final right" that the suffering body claims is different from the organic rightness of the sensual body in *A Sport of Nature*, though at another level they are both combined in the historical body to which any individual consciousness is fastened. Both Gordimer and Coetzee have wanted to signal towards a realm "where bodies are their own signs",[33] if only because they have been immersed in a culture in which bodies have been seen as totally classifiable by signifying systems. In the trajectory of Coetzee's fiction, which in this respect has been opposite to Gordimer's, he has not further problematized the historical subject but gradually granted it more power, just as he has gradually granted narrative-as opposed to meta-narrative-more power, so that *Age of Iron* is the least interrupted and problematized of his narratives and is also cast in a most intimate familial form, a letter from mother to daughter. Mrs Curren, unlike Magda in In the *Heart of the Country*, does not doubt her own ontological status. By making the handing over of her letter an act of trust (trust in an "outcast" figure, which always makes a basic human claim on charity, a different claim than that made by the young "terrorist" John, but related), Coetzee draws attention to the "trust in the other and in the future... at the ethical heart of the situation" in South Africa in 1986 and in the "acute ethico-political trauma of the postcolonial world".[34] In this procedure, by making his narrative both monologue and love letter, he also reinstalls the irreplaceable subjectivities involved in communicative acts, which cannot be reduced to textuality, and reaffirms an intersubjectivity sometimes called love.[35] From one point of view, the significant subjectivity we "white" readers recognize in Mrs Curren as we read her letter to her daughter is as valuable as the significant subjectivity we recognize in those "black" readers and speakers who will read it and respond differently, even though the latter inhabit historical bodies as Mrs Curren and her daughter do not. Our engagement with the voices of fiction is also an ethical and imaginative process.

What, then, might the implications of all of this be for the Canadian contested zone of postmodernism and postcolonialism? Diana Brydon has argued that "there are several Canadian post-modernisms just as there is more than one Canadian postcolonial voice."[36] Frank Davey has outlined with great clarity what those different Canadian postmodernisms look like, as well as the critical positions from which they have been challenged. He argues that his own earlier version of postmodernism was deployed on behalf of "decentralized politics" and on "a field of colonial-imperial relations".[37] Like Brydon, he emphasizes that "the word is anything but an unproblematic, uncontradictory, and totalizable sign,"[38] though this is the way some postcolonial critics have positioned it, as the sign of the merely aesthetic, of free play, of a totalized Europe or international capitalism. He sees Robert Kroetsch as promoting a "political postmodern-a postmodern that is postcolonial, specifically "Canadian, but can also serve to legitimate the Canadian west".[39] Kroetsch has affinities with Coetzee, then, in using postmodern strategies to promote a postcolonial, yet also regional and national, awareness of difference by signalling the difficulties of representing difference within ideologically loaded genres. One way of deconstructing myths is to go "back to the specifics, the occasions of narrative".[40] Paradoxically, it seems that in the specifics of narrative, that labyrinth of voice which subtends individual and communal identity, overarching national identities and European as well as Eurocentric canons and assumptions are deconstructed while a national literature is simultaneously redirected from within.[41]

Notes

1. This article is a review article of the two following books: Bruce King, ed. *The Later Fiction of Nadine Gordiner*. Basingstoke, Macmillan, 1993. pp.x, 249. David Attwell. *J. M. Coetzee: South Africa and the Politics of Writing*, University of California P, 1993. pp. ix, 147.

2. Glenn, in "Nadine Gordimer, J. M. Coetzee, and the Politics of Interpretation," traces these debates and conflicts very fully in terms of Bourdieu's model of struggles for dominance in literary fields.

3. See Annamaria Carusi's "Post, Post and Post. Or, Where is South African Literature in All This?" and the October 1993 issue of *Current Writing* from the University of Natal, Durban.

4. See Teresa Dovey's *The Novels of J.M. Coetzee: Lacanian Allegories.*

5. As Paul A. Cantor suggests, much is to be learned by repoliticizing our view of writers such as Beckett and Joyce. "These two authors take on new meaning when understood as in some sense postcolonial.... It may turn out that postcolonialism is the more fundamental phenomenon and that we will succeed in tracing many of the features of literature that we now label 'postmodern' to the postcolonial situation of so many authors of this century, including some Europeans" (103).

6. See Dorothy Driver's "Nadine Gordimer: The Politicization of Women".

7. Coetzee *Doubling* 341-42.

8. Carusi 96.

9. King 3.

10. Gordimer *Sport* 102, 328, quoted in Cooke 27.

11. Greenstein, quoted in King 201.

12. King 33-44.

13. Ibid 45-58.

14. Smith 57.

15. King 124.

16. Ibid 74-88.

17. Ibid 86.

18. Gordimer *Selected* 12.

19. Gordimer *Essential* 267.

20. What such a critique might sound like was illustrated at the 1994 CACLALS conference in Calgary by a graduate student from Ghana, Yaw Asante, who argued that Gordimer's *July's People* "actually insists on a cultural and racial superiority" for white South Africans.

21. Coetzee *Doubling* 341.

22. This and the following point were made in conversation with the author at the December 1993 MLA, at lunch in a pleasant neo-colonial hotel.

23. Attwell 3.

24. Ibid 5.

25. Ibid 6.

26. Ibid 125.

27. Coetzee *Heart*, quoted in *Cantor* 91, 101.

28. Hutcheon 2.

29. Rody 162.

30. Wood 194.

31. During 28.

32. Coetzee *Doubling* 248.

33. Coetzee *Foe* 157.

34. Attridge 66,76.

35. A strange but fairly typical South African family is reconstituted in *Age of Iron*: an unreliable secretly drinking lower-class (Afrikaner) father, a liberal English middle-class mother, a politically radical (black) son, and an exiled (white) daughter. Given that Coetzee says that the novel is about messengers and heralds, it is interesting that the family message will only be carried from mother to daughter if the unreliable father/messenger is faithful beyond death. He has to be trusted because he is all there is to trust. And if fathers are not to be trusted, what is left? But trust seems to be the sine qua non of the family and the new South African order.

36. Brydon 194.

37. Davey 251.

38. Ibid 254.

39. Ibid 255.

40. Kroetsch, quoted in Neuman 92, and in Davey 256.

41. Such narratives are not necessarily only postmodern. Helen Hoy argues persuasively in "Discursive Transparency in Beatrice Culleton" that a Canadian text as apparently representational, even documentary, as *In Search of April Raintree* needs to have the duplicity of its craft acknowledged, that "it both invites and disrupts notions of the real and of the self, of authenticity and of identity, of truth" (179). Hoy's argument has implications for Linda Hutcheon's assertion that Native and Métis writers in Canada "should be considered the resisting, postcolonial voice of Canada" ("Circling the Downspout" 72); so does Lee Maracle's assertion that postcolonialism has no meaning for us whatsoever, which is why it never comes up in discourse

between us. We're still fighting classical colonialism" (Kelly 83). Canada has been without South Africa's forms of external and internal colonialism, but also without its more decisively liberating postcolonial moments for Afrikaner and black. Colonial, neo-colonial, and postcolonial strands are more diffusely plaited throughout the fabric of Canadian society and literature. An exchange of views on postcolonial studies and their relevance in Canada features in the first issue of *Arachne*, from Laurentian University.

Posting South African Letters from Canada

"Between sleep and dream, The I am and what I am, And who I think I am, A river runs for ever." – (David Wright, "Between Sleep and Dream, After Fernando Pessoa")

"And when we got to Rock Fort we seemed to look over everything out to the satisfying sea." – (John Figueroa, "Growing Up in Jamaica")

South African "letters" have not yet been very thoroughly "posted" within the main cluster of national literatures usually grouped under the umbrella of post-colonialism. This has everything to do with the establishment of the Republic in 1961, South Africa's expulsion from the Commonwealth and the implementation of apartheid which conferred pariah status on the country for so long. From a more highly theorized Western viewpoint, or even from other "Second World" sites,[1] South African literary culture was at first seen as a significant and troubling exception to the implicit and explicit norms set up, for instance, in *The Empire Writes Back* (1989), the first compendium of post-colonial theory.[2] First phase postcolonial theory generally posited a progressive cultural drive towards an emancipated post-colonial world as the central feature of post-colonial writing, despite counter-arguments concerning the implied historical progression from colonialism to post-colonialism.[3] When such studies appeared, South Africa had not yet achieved a democratic system of political representation, and some critics felt the "post" appellation was premature in a pre-democratic situation, before any "imagined community of South Africa (could) begin to approach identification with the state".[4] Ashcroft et al. argued that racist politics in South Africa "creates a political vortex into which much of the literature of the area, both black

146

and white, is drawn".[5] They also assumed that the common themes of most post-colonial writing are "muted" by racial politics in South Africa.[6] The troubling implication was that the literatures of other settler colonies have less to do with "race politics",[7] that South Africa has been a disquieting exception to a norm. This assumption indicates the extent to which post-colonial theory has sometimes abstracted itself from the disturbing world of the actual inequalities with which we live, created by many forms of imperialism usually coterminous with forms of racism.[8] It also indicates that post-colonial theory itself, and attitudes toward theory, are determined by the cultural politics of origin. Critiques emanating from the racially oppressed in South Africa, for instance, have tended to stress the continuity of effects flowing from apartheid,[9] just as African writer Chinua Achebe has wanted to hold on to a sense of the damage and distortion flowing from colonialism in Africa and its culturally biased expression and reception in literature.[10] The moralized view of art, of literature as the handmaiden of social change, has been an African tradition. In this respect, South African culture has some affinities with the rest of Africa.[11]

To change countries, as I did when immigrating from South Africa to Canada in 1991, is to recognize quite sharply and repeatedly the extent to which a past self has been socially constructed by a particular culture, and to recognize anew the deep consolations and commonalities which literature offers in reconstituting a self in another country. The literature of immigration within the colonial and post-colonial worlds has acquired a far more profound and sustaining meaning for me, as have the critical writings of diasporic intellectuals or expatriate writers. Thus I am led to a renewed investment in an experiencing self, that same self who makes a continuing commitment to feminist perspectives, while acknowledging that shifting to Canadian perspectives has made notions of identity and nation problematic and ambiguous, like language. "Rhetorical estrangement," argues Rei Terada in a study of Derek Walcott, "can be taken for granted in all language",[12] since "writing... substitutes figuration for presence... and marks the site of perpetually abandoned presence".[13]

In this zone of a double abandonment, where language rushes in to fill the spaces of loss and simultaneously creates a new ambivalence, South Africa, in its incontestable and flagrant racial injustice, has always seemed to offer a kind of "limit case" for post-colonial theory. Yet, paradoxically, it offered an "affirmative case... the one stable element in our thinking".[14] The current decade of post-apartheid revision has included many forms of re-assessment. In 1992, a special issue of *Current Writing* featured the intersections of post-colonial theory and South African literary culture. The problematic relationship of South African political dispensations and the gross inequities of a racially-ordered economy to international theory were discussed from the new perspectives of the nineties. There was an awareness of the colonially constructed critical establishment, the problematic domination of the critical forum by minority white voices, a post-modern theorizing of difference and self-reflexivity which did not assume that post-modernism was necessarily inimical to the element of political protest so often foregrounded in South African literature.[15] The often polarized and stagnant debate between a detached aesthetic and a call for political commitment in literature[16] was thrown open to new voices and a melange of theoretical standpoints. South African critics, Kelwyn Sole later suggested, should begin to close the gap between "high" and "popular" forms, a call in South Africa that usually implies a closer understanding of the relationship between literature and oral tradition.[17] Formulations of this relationship have become increasingly sophisticated, drawing in local knowledges and research, and developing perceptions of the renewal and reworking of orality in modern texts and performances within a politicized environment.[18]

In Canada, with an understanding of both the South African political experience and the diasporic sense of dislocation in a northern, multicultural society, Rosemary Jolly has made the international reception of South African theatre a foil for revealing the constructedness of international post-colonial theory itself, its dangers and special investments. The controversial preface written by Derrida for an anti-apartheid art exhibition, she writes, is guilty of a "spectacular othering" of South Africa,[19] and is neo-colonial in effect. Derrida invites condemnation of apartheid as an atrocity, and thus "turns the reader's critical gaze away from American and European colonialism".[20] Derrida's preface dates from 1983, and seems at first a Gallic rhetorical gesture towards the inevitable imbrication of political action in language. While in some ways it may seem to offend a post-Marxist desire to connect the materiality of politics to cultural expression,[21] it does at least point out that "the stability of the Pretoria regime has been prerequisite to the political, economic and strategic equilibrium of Europe."[22] This identification of global, capitalist interdependence lays the ground for a post-apartheid insight that has some applicability across Africa: the crumbling of internal settler colonialism has not meant the withdrawal of economic control.[23] A relative separation of the economic and cultural spheres is potentially liberating, allowing for views of cultural agency, for people's self-assertion and a more positive view of the creative use of the English language by those not born into it.[24]

Apartheid is graphically described by Derrida as a projection of Europe's inner contradictions, "the double-bind logic of its national and multinational interests".[25] This has the virtue of restoring the South African political scene to a global context of colonialism and capitalism. Derrida's preface, in 1983, raised the problem of the limits of humanist discourse and the relationship of that discourse to the denunciation of apartheid. It traverses post-modernist ground in its final collapse of chronology as it appeals to "the future of another law and another force lying beyond the totality of the present".[26] The paintings, he suggests, create a memory of the future and in their silence appeal to a justice beyond discourse. This complex invocation does anticipate post-apartheid discussions of the problematic relation of memory and forgetting in South Africa.

In a special 1996 edition of *Ariel*, which I edited, a number of different critics, South African, Canadian, and returned exiles, suggested ways of rereading South African literature and culture in the nineties. All of them are responding to the challenge articulated by Njabulo Ndebele in 1989: "the search for ways of thinking, ways of perception, that will help to break down the closed epistemological structures of South African oppression... to free the entire social imagination of the oppressed from the laws of perception that have characterized apartheid society."[27] Frank Schulze-Engler argued for pluralist perspectives and civil society accountability, and showed how these spaces were being created in the fictions of Gordimer and Coetzee. Simon Lewis's reading of Cecil Rhodes and Olive Schreiner's inscriptions of Europe in Africa by way of their imposing gravesites and death rituals of-

fered a novel conjunction of two figures previously seen as ideologically opposed. Lewis showed how they both laid claim to the land and
to African identity, and naturalized European presences as African.
Karen Blixen's account of her lover, Finch-Hatton's death, Lewis describes as "Imperial Gothic".[28] (This term could be appropriated for
Margaret Atwood's novel, *Alias Grace*, though here Imperial Gothic
is being ironically scrutinized and dismembered, so to speak). Lewis's
reading of the sentimentality of these cultural rituals, not to mention
their appropriation of the best African viewsites, is a timely reminder of the ways in which colonial viewpoints have been uncritically
received as normative because of continued European hegemony in
education and critical institutions. It may be too soon to rejoice in
our deconstructed perspectives; Sally-Ann Murray's superb analysis
of Sol Kerzner's themed resort north of Johannesburg, "The Lost City,"
shows how Tarzan and Rider Haggard are not yet dead, but alive and
well and making millions for entrepreneurs and their shareholders.
Murray reads "The Lost City" as "the repressed 'heart of darkness' of
the South African urban nexus",[29] and shows how it blurs distinctions
between entertainment and commodity, history and fiction.[30] In a fine
example of cultural studies in South Africa, she suggests that the resort stages one form of fabricated national identity and shows that
colonialism was never a monolithic project. Nor will its traces ever
disappear, it seems. She also argues that there are no simple ideological meanings to be read off the project. There is no single, authentic South African cultural tradition to invoke. This decentred view of
identity and nation echoes the recommendations of Albie Sachs that
if South African artists and writers cease to submit their imaginations
to the dictates of cultural commissars they will find access to many
shared South African traditions.[31] Murray suggests a process of reconstruction across different idioms, not all of which will be conducive
to democratization. Capitalism did not disappear along with the dismantling of apartheid laws, and the new political dispensation, now
perceived as the neo-liberal result of a negotiated settlement, disturbs
any easy sense of a cultural millennium.[32]

In "Writing the New South Africa," a number of critics suggest,
however, that a more tolerant and open atmosphere for artistic creation has emerged, whether in a rapprochement of private and pub-

lic voices in poetry,[33] or the courageous emergence of "gay" writing, which reveals the far-reaching damage done by the workings of patriarchy and the military control of the racist order.[34] Heyns's article on "erotic patriarchy" raises the central question of the extent to which local conditions, and South African nationalisms, affect the critical reading of archetypal patterns in literature and of international theory. The construction of subjectivity through colonial ideology is given an autobiographical format by Devarakshanam Govinden, who recalls her own construction as a Leavisite, and sees in her earlier romance with English literature the workings of colonialism in collusion with apartheid. Her article, which refers to Toni Morrison and V.S. Naipaul, among others, begins to suggest ways of reading gender, educational construction and colonialism in other countries in the ex-Commonwealth. In Canada, too, a romance with English literature has served different ideological ends, both the remembering of ethnic heritages and the partial obscuring of Canadian political formations.[35] Rob Gaylard's analysis of Zoe Wicomb's short stories invokes post-colonial comparisons to Jamaica Kincaid and Michelle Cliff in the shared problems of hybridized identity and writing about home from exile. Such comparative studies of gender and postcolonialism would be a useful response to Robert Robertson's request for "a recovery of the comparative approach" in post-colonial studies.[36] Gender and subjectivity are also related critical categories in the work of Judith Coullie and Margaret Daymond on South African autobiographies and short stories. Coullie's work is sensitive to the African communal traditions that underpin African women's subjectivity, but also suggests that fluid forms of reciprocity and shared self-definition are evident in white South African women's autobiographical writing. This extension of genre begins to suggest the breaking down of racial categories in critical description. So, too, do Margaret Daymond's conclusions that recent reworkings of the short story show women's subjectivity having "significant public consequences".[37] Unlike earlier oppositions set up between gender and anti-racist allegiances, now it is "through their gendered selves" that these writers produce "women's vital, creative relationship to their past".[38]

Dennis Walder's recent overview of *Postcolonial Literatures in English* (1998) takes South Africa as one case history precisely because it troubles "any simple notions of post-colonial literatures in English".[39] This is partly because of the intransigence of apartheid structures and thought, but also because the South African diaspora created another, outside presence, more or less politicized. The return of some exiles has led to new perspectives, such as that of Mbulelo Mzamane, who argues that democracy is only shallowly established in South Africa, that the real "writing" is in a sense deferred by the pressing problems of land claims, poverty, education and illiteracy. Like Nkosi and Ndebele, he tends to homogenize and dismiss black South African fiction as "protest fiction" and suggests that a turn to interiority will be a feature of new work.[40] Black South African fiction deserves more consideration and analysis than such summary dismissals allow. As Dennis Walder points out, post-apartheid South Africa may be most important for the mingling of a new sense of community values and a post-structuralist sense that the meaning of difference is unstable.[41] Like Mzamane and Ndebele, Walder sees the 1976 watershed of the schoolchildren's revolution as a potentially hopeful inauguration of new trends in literature and power-sharing. He singles out Gordimer's *The Conservationist* (1974) and J. M. Coetzee's *Dusklands* (1974) as marking a crisis in the "way the colonial imagination deals with the reality it perceives".[42]

One of the encouraging aspects of the lifting of cultural boycotts that accompanied the transition to democracy in South Africa has been the greater engagement between South African and African intellectuals. Conferences and publications linking cultural studies, women's studies and post-colonialism have highlighted the crucial topics of the nineties: the boundary of local and imperial knowledge in interdisciplinary models; the relationship of material culture and textuality; a testing of the totalizing power of theoretical discourse against local knowledge; an applied politics of usage and context; a shifting of language, culture and subjectivity to the centre of theory and analysis; integrating the study of culture with the history of capitalism; listening to colonized voices and subjugated knowledges, and understanding forms of rupture and continuity between colonialism and post-colonialism.[43]

These intersecting topics are as important for the study of postcolonialism in Canada, where a multicultural society, the tension between English Canada and the claims of Quebec, and multiple immigrant and ethnic histories make an understanding of and sensitivity to difference crucial. Political claims and resistance are dispersed across a number of competing sites in Canadian culture, and thus make any monolithic assertion of nation or cultural meaning impossible. The constant process of immigrant absorption and the tension between assimilation and difference give Canadian culture its characteristic qualities. Literature in Canada plays an increasingly important role in the understanding of difference as critical focus has shifted away from relationships between settlers and landscape, and stereotypes or images of communities, to an understanding of constantly shifting differences, constructed against one another, to what Kamboureli has called "contamination" and "ambivalence".[44] This post-modern emphasis co-exists with calls for a more historicized postcolonialism in Canada.[45]

The history of immigration in Canada has produced a diversity of critical positions within post-colonialism itself. Canadians of European origin tend to stress their ambivalence: "we occupy an ambivalent position within the postcolonial dynamic."[46] Critics in Canada with "Third World" cultural backgrounds have enacted a more complex trajectory in rejecting their own induction into Western theoretical models as universal models, and in questioning the racial exclusions of earlier feminism in North America.[47] Such critical positioning has meant a clearer recognition of, and a felt affiliation with anti-apartheid struggles in South Africa. Arun Mukherjee has argued for the recognition of a more directly politicized, post-colonial critique and pedagogy. She suggested that it is important whether or not we believe Miriam Tlali's accounts of township life to be true, because the reception of her fictions was important in conditioning political responses to South Africa from an outside constituency.[48] This sympathy with the actuality of South African resistance struggles has also been a force within some Canadian fiction, as in Lee Maracle's *Sundogs* (1992). A double metaphor, in the text and in a painting by a young First Nations girl, links the forms of solidarity created across cultures:

> A solitary black woman, sweet and innocent, silhouetted over an indigenous woman, also young and innocent, are in the foreground.

Behind them the illusion of crowds and picket signs, with no writing on them, makes the background. Both women are rich in colour... "What are the people doing?" "Protesting." "What are they protesting?" "Apartheid."[49]

This is one Canadian textual moment contributing to a "diaspora of postcolonial response" to South African political struggles in which the tropes of resistance have been mobilized and harnessed to an internal emancipatory struggle.[50]

Reading South African literature and post-colonialism from Canada allows the emergence of comparative perspectives which in turn link to a perception of "the historicity of Commonwealth literature".[51] G.N. Devi suggests that "Commonwealth literature has been a literary period in the history of Australian or Canadian literature,"[52] but the development of a "commonwealth consciousness" has "indirectly contributed to the emergence of a pan-Indian literary identity".[53] Such a consciousness creates a link with an international audience, builds cultural self-confidence and furthers resistance to "the new imperialism of literary theory".[54] Edwin Thumboo uses the Singaporean model of a multiracial, multi-lingual and multicultural society to set literature's subversions against the questionable "universal values" of "great literature." Against the neo-colonial claim of universality he sets "the process that defines the work in terms of a particular social semiotic, one that may be quite different and even subverting of the reader's own".[55] In contrast to the postmodern notion of migrancy, Satendra Nandan argues that "the migrant was and is a non-negotiable reality of the Pacific environment."[56] Coups in Fiji, as in Nigeria, have brutalized "the developing political culture".[57] In such environments, writers can assist readers to "recognize the reality itself".[58] Post-colonial writers, Stephen Slemon has suggested, continue to find ways to write their societies, and in doing so render visible "the dynamic operations of a persisting textual hegemony in colonial and postcolonial areas".[59] Wilson Harris coins the more encouraging phrase "inner objectivity" to describe a principle that may perhaps take reader and writer through the "comedy of coincidence" and through "cruel legacies, cruel bias" to an "impossible survival".[60]

Notes

1. See Lawson "Cultural".

2. Subsequently, two readers in Post-colonial Theory have appeared, one edited by Williams and Chrisman, (1993) and the other by Ashcroft, Griffiths and Tiffin (1995).

3. As Donna Bennett points out: "Postcolonialism internalizes an evolutionary model; it envisions a passing through progressive stages of unfreedom to freedom and of blindness to enlightenment" (195).

4. Voss 8.

5. Ashcroft *Empire* 27.

6. Ibid.

7. Ibid.

8. For a canvassing of the types of racial and cultural exclusions found in constructions of Canadian literature and post-colonial theory, see Arun Mukherjee's essay "Canadian Nationalism, Canadian Literature, and Racial Minority Literature" in *Essays on Canadian Writing*, vol. 56, pp. 78-95.

9. See Mzamane "Resistance"; Govinden "Memory".

10. See Achebe *Hopes*.

11. See Chapman *Southern*; Sole "Democratizing".

12. Terada 7.

13. Ibid 220.

14. Bhabha, Attwell interview, 111.

15. See Bethlehem "In/Articulation".

16. See De Kock "Heart".

17. See Sole "Democratizing"

18. See Gunner *Politics*; Hofmeyr *Spend*.

19. Jolly "Rehearsals" 19.

20. Ibid.

21. Bundy "Sharing" 33.

22. Derrida "Racism's" 295.

23. Gikandi *Reading* 113.

24. Robert T. Robertson, in his introduction to *A Shaping of Connections* (1989), sees the explosion of the English language all over the world as an enlargement of the social world in which "place became more important than period" in literary study (6). Neil ten Kortenaar also stresses the ways in which communities narrate

their place in the world by showing how Achebe's *Arrow of God* "offers possibilities for collective self-definition and action" (40).

25. Derrida "Racism's" 298.

26. Ibid 298.

27. Ndebel "Redefining".

28. Lewis "Graves" 50.

29. Murray "Tropes" 155.

30. Ibid 151.

31. See Sachs "Preparing".

32. See Murray *Revolution*.

33. See De Kock "Heart"

34. See Heyns "Fathers".

35. The Special Issue of *Essays on Canadian Writing*, vol. 57, "Writing Ethnicity," highlights many of these ways of reading "the category of ethnicity itself as a meeting ground of often conflicting desires and investments" (Siemerling, Introduction, 2).

36. Robertson "Hussites" 7.

37. Daymond *South* 210.

38. Ibid. M.J. Daymond's edition of *South African Feminisms* reveals the evolution of these debates about gender and race in South African feminism.

39. Walder *Post-Colonial* 154.

40. Mzamane "Resistance" 11,18. An unfortunate precedent was created by Lewis Nkosi's wholesale dismissal of South African fiction by black writers in *Home and Exile* (1965), one reproduced by Ndebele in some of his work and also by Mzamane in "Writing the New South Africa." All of them elide substantial differences in this body of work, as well as the contributions of women writers.

41. Walder *Post-Colonial* 156-158.

42. Ibid 165.

43. See Werbner *Postcolonial*.

44. Kamboureli "Signifying" 231-2.

45. See Bennett "English"; McDonald "Looked".

46. Brydon "Response" 101.

47. See Mukherjee *Oppositional*.

48. See Mukherjee "Whose".

49. Maracle *Sundogs* 72-73.

50. I owe this useful phrase to Donna Palmateer Pennee.

51. Devi *Commonwealth* 59.

52. Ibid.

53. Ibid 61.

54. Ibid.

55. Thumboo "Commonwealth" 66.

56. Nandan "Beyond" 69.

57. Ibid.

58. Ibid 70.

59. Slemon "Reading" 120.

60. Harris "Comedy" 128-133.

Selected Bibliography

Abrahams, Peter. *Mine Boy*. Heinemann,1946.

Abrahams, Peter. *Wild Conquest*. Faber, 1951.

Achebe, Chinua. *Anthills of the Savannah*. Heinemann,1987.

Achebe, Chinua. *Arrow of God*. Heinemann, 1964.

Achebe, Chinua. "Colonialist Criticism." *Hopes and Impediments: Selected Essays 1965-87*. London: Heinemann, 1988.

Achebe, Chinua. *Hopes and Impediments: Selected Essays 1965-87*. Heinemann, 1988.

Achebe, Chinua. *A Man of the People*. Heinemann, 1966.

Achebe, Chinua. *No Longer at Ease*. Heinemann, 1960

Achebe, Chinua. *Things Fall Apart*. Heinemann, 1958.

Adam, Heribert. *Modernizing Racial Domination: The Dynamics of South African Politics*. University of California Press, 1971.

Adam, Ian, et al, editors. *Past the Last Post: Theorizing Post-Colonialism and Post Modernism*. University of Calgary Press, 1990.

Alcoff, Linda Martin. "The Politics of Postmodern Feminism, Revisited." *Cultural Critique*, vol. 36, 1997, pp. 5-28.

Alexander, Ruth. "Review of S.C. Conwright-Schreiner's *The Life of Olive Schreiner*." *The South African Nation*, vol. 9, 1924.

Alpers, Antony. *The Life of Katherine Mansfield*. Oxford University Press, 1982.

Armah, Ayi Kwei. *The Beautyful Ones Are Not Yet Born*. Houghton Mifflin Harcourt, 1968

Armah, Ayi Kwei. *Fragments.* Heinemann, 1970.

Asante, Yaw. "What Is So Special About 'White Skin'? Or, Who's Afraid of Nadine Gordimer? The '(Other) Category' in *July's People." Chimo*, vol. 28, 1994, pp. 9-11.

Ashcroft, Bill, et al. *The Empire Writes Back: Theory and Practice in Post-Colonial Literatures,* Routledge, 1989.

Ashcroft, Bill, et al. *The Post-Colonial Studies Reader.* Routledge, 1995.

Attridge, Derek. "Trusting the Other: Ethics and Politics in J. M. Coetzee's *Age of Iron." The Writings of J.M. Coetzee.* Michael Valdez Moses, editor. Special issue of *South Atlantic Quarterly*, vol. 93, no. 1, 1994, pp. 59-82.

Attwell, David. "Introduction." *Current Writing*, vol. 5, no. 2, 1993, pp. 1-6.

Attwell, David. "Interview with Homi Bhabha." *Current Writing*, vol. 5, no. 2, 1993, pp. 100-113.

Atwood, Margaret. *Alias Grace.* McLelland & Stewart, 1996.

Atwood, Margaret. *Surfacing.* McClelland and Stewart, 1972.

Awoonor, Kofi. *Comes the Voyager at Last.* Africa World Press, 1992

Behr, Mark. *The Smell of Apples.* Abacus, 1995.

Bennett, Donna. "English Canada's Postcolonial Complexities." *Essays on Canadian Writing*, vol. 51-52, 1993-4, pp. 164-210.

Bethlehem, Louise Shabat. "In/Articulation: Polysystem. Theory, Postcolonial Discourse Theory, and South African Literary Historiography." *Current Writing*, vol. 5, no. 2, 1993, pp. 25-43.

Black Mamba Rising: South African Worker Poets in Struggle. Worker Resistance and Cultural Productions, 1986.

Boehmer, Elleke. "What Will They Read Now? The Loosening of the Novel After the struggle Against Apartheid." *Times Literary Supplement*, April 1994, pp. 10-11.

Brown, Mary. "Recollections of Olive Schreiner" in *The Life of Mrs John Brown.* Edited by Angela James et al. John Murray, 1937, pp.183-205.

Brown, Susan, et al. *LIP from Southern African Women*. Ravan, 1983.

Brydon, Diana. "Response to Hart." *Arachne*, vol. 1, no. 1, 1994, pp. 100-112.

Brydon, Diana. "The White Inuit Speaks: Contamination as Literary Strategy." Adam, Ian, et al, editors. *Past the Last Post: Theorizing Post-Colonialism and Post Modernism*. University of Calgary Press, 1990. pp. 191-203.

Buang Basadi. COSAW Journal – Special Issue on Women and Writing Conference. 1988.

Bundy, Colin. "Sharing the Burden? A Response to Terry Lovell." *Transgressing Boundaries: New Directions in the Study of Culture in Africa*. Edited by Brenda Cooper et al. UCT Press, 1996. 31-38.

Cantor, Paul A. "Days in the Veld: Beckett and Coetzee's *In the Heart of the Country*." Special issue of *South Atlantic Quarterly*, vol. 93, no. 1, 1994,pp. 83-110.

Cartey, Wilfred. *Whispers from a Continent*. Heinemann, 1971.

Carusi, Annamaria. "Post, Post and Post. Or, Where is South African Literature in All This?" Adam, Ian, et al, editors. *Past the Last Post: Theorizing Post-Colonialism and Post Modernism*. University of Calgary Press, 1990.

Chapman, Michael. *Southern African Literatures*. Longman, 1996.

Cheney-Coker, Syl. *The Last Harmattan of Alusine Dunbar*. Pearson Education, 1990

Clayton Cherry, editor. *ARIEL: Writing the New South Africa*, vol. 27, no. 1, 1996.

Clayton, Cherry, editor. *Olive Schreiner*. McGraw Hill, 1983.

Clayton, Cherry. "Post-colonial, Post-apartheid, Post-feminist: Family and State in Prison Narratives by South African Women." New Art and Literature from South Africa. *International Journal of Canadian Studies / Revue Internationale D'études Canadiennes*. Kirsten Holst Petersen and Anna Rutherford, editors. Aarhus: Kunapipi, 1991. 136-144.

Clayton, Cherry, editor. *Women and Writing in South Africa: A Critical Anthology*. Heinemann, 1989.

Clingman, R. *The Novels of Nadine Gordimer: History from the Inside*. Ravan, 1986.

Clingman, R. *Doubling the Point: Essays and Interviews*. Edited by David Attwell. Harvard University Press, 1992.

Coetzee, J.M. *Age of Iron*. Secker & Warburg, 1990.

Coetzee, J.M. *Dusklands*. Ravan, 1974.

Coetzee, J. M. *Foe*. Ravan, 1986.

Coetzee, J. M. *In the Heart of the Country*. Ravan, 1978.

Coetzee, J. M. *Life and Times of Michael K*. Ravan, 1983.

Coetzee, J. M. *South Africa and the Politics of Writing*. University of California Press, 1993.

Coetzee, J. M. *Waiting for the Barbarians*. Ravan, 1981.

Coetzee, J. M. *White Writing: On the Culture of Letters in South Africa*. Radix; Yale University Press, 1988.

Collingwood, R.G. *The Idea of History*. Clarendon Press, 1946.

Cronwright-Schreiner, S.C. *The Re-interment on Buffelskop*. 1921. Edited by Butler, Guy. Institute for the Study of English in Africa, Rhodes University, 1983.

Conwright-Schreiner, S.C. *The Life of Olive Schreiner*. Fisher Unwin, 1924.

Conwright-Schreiner, S.C. Introduction to *From Man to Man*. Fisher Unwin, 1926.

Cornwell, Gareth. "Evaluating Protest Fiction." *English in Africa,* vol. 7, no. 1, 1980, pp. 51-70.

Coullie, Judith Lütge. "(In)Continent I-Lands: Blurring the Boundaries Between Self and Other in South African Women's Autobiographies." *ARIEL,* vol. 27, no. 1, 1996, pp. 133-148.

Culleton, Beatrice. *In Search of April Raintree*. Pemmican, 1983.

Darby, Phillip. *The Fiction of Imperialism*. A&C Black, 1998.

Davey, Frank. "Contesting 'Post(-)modernism." *Canadian Literary Power, the Writer As Critic.* NeWest, 1994.

Davidson, Basil. *The Black Man's Burden.* Spectrum Books, 1992.

Davis, Charles T. *Black is the Colour of the Cosmos: Essays on Afro-American Literature and Culture 1942-1981.* Garland, 1982.

Davis, Nick. "Narrative Composition and the Spatial Memory." *Narrative: From Malory to Motion Pictures.* Edited by Jeremy Hawthorn. Arnold, 1985, pp. 25-40.

Daymond, M.J. "Gender and History: 1980s South African Women's Stories in English." *ARIEL,* vol. 27, no. 1, 1996, pp. 191-214.

Daymond, M.J. *South African Feminisms: Writing, Theory and Criticism, 1990-1994.* Garland Publishing, 1996.

DeKok, Ingrid. *Familiar Ground.* Ravan, 1988.

DeKok, Ingrid, et al. *Spring Is Rebellious: Arguments about Cultural Freedom by Albie Sachs and Respondents.* Buchu Books, 1990.

De Kock, Leon et al. "The Heart in Exile: South African Poetry in English,1990-95." *ARIEL,* vol. 27, no. 1, 1996, pp. 105-132.

Delaney, Lucy A. In William L. Andrews, *Six Women's Slave Narratives.* Oxford University Press, 1988.

Delius, Peter. *The Land Belongs to Us.* Ravan, 1983.

Derrida, Jacques. "Racism's Last Word." Translated by Peggy Kamuf. *Race Writing and Difference.* Henry Louis gates Jr., editor. University of Chicago Press, 1986, pp. 329-338.

Devi, G.N. "The Commonwealth Literature Period: A Note Towards the History of Indian English Literature." *A Shaping of Connections.* Edited by Hena Maes-Jelinek et al. Dangaroo Press, 1989. pp. 56-62.

Diamond, Arlyn, et al. *The Authority of Experience.* University of Massachusetts Press, 1977.

Dovey, Teresa. *The Novels of J.M. Coetzee: Lacanian Allegories.* Donker, 1988.

Driver, Dorothy, "Nadine Gordimer: The Politicization of Women." *English in Africa,* vol. 10, no. 2, 1983, pp. 29-54,

Driver, Dorothy. "'Woman' as Sign in the South African Colonial Enterprise." *Journal of Literary Studies*, vol. 4, no. 1, 1988, pp. 3-20.

Du Plessis, Menan. *A State of Fear.* David Philip, 1983.

Du Plessis, Menan. *Longlive.* David Philip, 1989.

During, Simon. "Waiting for The Post: Some Relations Between Modernity, Colonization, and Writing." Ian Adam et al, editors. *Past the Last Post: Theorizing Post-Colonialism and Post Modernism.* University of Calgary Press, 1990, pp. 23-45.

Emberley, Julia. *Feminist Critique, Native Women's Writings, Postcolonial Theory.* 1993.

Fairbridge, Dorothea. *A History of South Africa.* Oxford University Press, 1918.

Fanon, Frantz. *The Wretched of the Earth.* Penguin, 1961.

Farah, Nuruddin. *Sweet and Sour Milk.* Graywolf Press, 1992.

Fatton, Robert Jr. "Liberal Democracy in Africa." *Political Science Quarterly*, vol. 105, no. 3, 1990, pp. 455-473.

First, Ruth. *117 Days: An Account of Confinement and Interrogation under the South African Ninety-Day Detention Law.* Penguin, 1965.

First, Ruth, et al. *Olive Schreiner: A Biography.* André Deutsch, 1980.

Foucault, Michel. *Discipline and Punish: The Birth of the Prison.* Peregrine, 1975.

Fradkin, Betty McGinnis. "Olive Schreiner and Karl Pearson." *Quarterly Bulletin of the South African Library*, vol. 3, no. 4, 1977, pp. 84-93

Frank, Katherine. "Feminist Criticism and the African Novel." *African Literature Today*, vol. 4,1984, pp. 34-48.

Friedman, Marion. *Olive Schreiner: A Study in Latent Meanings.* Witwatersrand University Press, 1955.

Gardner, Susan. "Production under Drought Conditions." *Africa Insight,* vol. 15, no. 1, 1985, pp. 43-46.

Gaylard, Rob. "Exile and Homecoming: Identity in Zoe Wicomb's *You Can't Get Lost in Cape Town." ARIEL*, vol. 27, no. 1, 1996, pp. 177-190.

Gikandi, Simon. *Reading Chinua Achebe: Language and Ideology in Fiction.* James Currey, 1991.

Ginwala, Frene. "ANC Women: Their Strength in the Struggle." Work in Progress, 1986, pp. 10-14.

Glenn, Ian. "Nadine Gordimer, J. M. Coetzee, and the Politics of Interpretation." *he Writings of J.M. Coetzee.* Michael Valdez Moses, editor. Special issue of *South Atlantic Quarterly*, vol. 93, no. 1, 1994, pp. 1-32.

Gordimer, Nadine. *Burger's Daughter.* Jonathan Cape, 1979.

Gordimer, Nadine. *The Conservationist.* Cape, 1974.

Gordimer, Nadine. *The Essential Gesture: Writing, Politics and Places.* Edited by Stephen Clingman. Penguin, 1989.

Gordimer, Nadine. *July's People.* Cape, 1981.

Gordimer, Nadine. *My Son's Story.* Penguin, 1991.

Gordimer, Nadine. *Selected Stories.* Penguin, 1983.

Gordimer, Nadine. *A Sport of Nature.* Cape, 1987.

Gould, Vera Buchanan. *Not Without Honour: The Life and Writings of Olive Schreiner.* Hutchinson, 1948.

Govinden, Devarakshanam. "Memory is a Weapon: Reading Under Apartheid." *ARIEL*, vol. 27, no. 1, 1996, pp. 215-230.

Gunner, Liz. *Politics and Performance: Theatre, Poetry and Songs in Southern Africa.* Witwatersrand University Press, 1994.

Gusdorf, Georges. "Conditions and Limits of Autobiography." *Autobiography.* Edited by James Olney. Princeton University Press, 1980.

Hanson, Clare, et al. *Katherine Mansfield.* Macmillan, 1981.

Harlow, Barbara. *Resistance Literature.* Methuen, 1987.

Harris, Wilson. "Comedy and Modern Allegory: A Personal View." *A Shaping of Connections.* Hena Maes-Jelinek et al., editors. Dangaroo Press, 1989, pp. 127-140.

Harrow, Kenneth. *Thresholds of Change in African Literature: The Emergence of Tradition.* 1994.

Hart, Jonathan. "Circling the Downspout of Empire." Adam, Ian, et al, editors. *Past the Last Post: Theorizing Post-Colonialism and Post Modernism*. University of Calgary Press, 1990, pp. 167-89.

Hart, Jonathan. "Perspectives on Postcolonial Theories." (Responses by Brian Shaffer and Diana Brydon.) *Arachne*, vol. 11, 1994, pp. 68-119.

Head, Bessie. *A Bewitched Crossroad*. Ad. Donker, 1984.

Head, Bessie. *The Collector of Treasures*. Heinemann, 1977.

Head, Bessie. Foreword to Ellen Kuzwayo's *Call Me Woman*. Ravan, 1985.

Head, Bessie. Foreword to *Native Life in South Africa*.

Head, Bessie. "Let Me Tell a Story Now..." *The New African*, 1962.

Head, Bessie. "Letter from South Africa." *Transition*, vol. 3, no. 11, 1963, p.40.

Head, Bessie. *Maru*. Heinemann, 1971.

Head, Bessie. *A Question of Power*. Heinemann, 1974.

Head, Bessie. *Serowe: Village of the Rain Wind*. Heinemann, 1981.

Head, Bessie. "Some Notes on Novel Writing," *New Classic*, vol.5, 1978, pp. 30-32.

Head, Bessie. "Writing out of Southern Africa." *New Statesman*, vol. 16, 1985, pp. 21-23..

Heyns, Michiel. "Fathers and Sons: Structures of Erotic Patriarchy in Afrikaans Writing of the Emergency." *ARIEL*, vol. 27, no. 1, 1996, pp. 81-104.

Heywood, Christopher. "Traditional Values in the Novels of Bessie Head." *Individual and Community in Commonwealth Literature*. Edited by Daniel Massa. Malta University Press, 1979, pp. 12-19.

Hobman, D.L. *Olive Schreiner: Her Friends and Times*. Watts & Co., 1955.

Hofmeyr, Isabel. "Kelwyn Sole, Postmodernism, and the Challenge of the Local." *Current Writing*, vol. 6, no. 2, 1994, pp. 49-52.

Hofmeyr, Isabel. *We Spend Our Years as a Tale that is Told: Oral Historical Narrative in a South African Chiefdom*. Witwatersrand University Press, 1993.

Howells, Coral Anne. *Private and Fictional Worlds: Canadian Women Novelists of the 1970s and 1980s.* Methuen, 1987.

Hoy, Helen. "Discursive Transparency in Beatrice Culleton." *ARIEL*, vol. 25, no. 1, 1994, pp. 155-184..

Huggan, Isabel. *You Never Know.* Knopf Canada, 1996

Hutcheon, Linda. T*he Canadian Postmodern: A Study of Contemporary English-Canadian Fiction.* University of Toronto Press, 1989.

JanMohamed, Abdul R. *Manichean Aesthetics.* University of Massachusetts Press, 1983.

Jolly, Rosemary. "Rehearsals of Liberation: Contemporary Postcolonial Discourse and the New South Africa." *PMLA*, vol. 110, no.1, 1995, no.17-29.

Jones, K.E. "In Defense of Rebecca Schreiner." *Forum,* vol. 4, no. 3, 1955, pp. 38-40.

Joubert, Elsa. *The Long Journey of Poppie Nongena.* Jonathan Ball, 1980.

Kaarsholm, Preben. "Lutheranism and Imperialism in the Novels of Olive Schreiner." *Kultur og Samfund.* Institut VI, Roskilde Universitetscenter, 1983.

Kamboureli, Smaro, "Signifying Contamination: On Austin Clarke's *Nine Men Who Laughed.*" *Essays on Canadian Writing*, vol. 57, 1995, pp. 212-234.

Karl, F.R. *Three Lives.* Faber & Faber, 1979.

Kelly, Jennifer. "Coming out of the House: A Conversation with Lee Maracle." *ARIEL*, vol. 25, no. 1, 1994, pp. 73-88.

King, Bruce, editor. *The Later Fiction of Nadine Gordimer.* Macmillan, 1993.

Kuzwayo, Ellen. *Call Me Woman.* Ravan, 1985.

Larson, Charles. *The Emergence of African Fiction.* Indiana University Press, 1972.

Laurence, Margaret. *The Prophet's Camel Bell.* 1963

Laurence, Margaret. *This Side of Jordan.* 1960

Laurence, Margaret. *The Tomorrow-Tamer and Other Storie*s. 1963.

Lawson, Alan. "A Cultural Paradigm for the Second World." *Australian-Canadian Studies*, vol. 9, no. 1-2, 1991, pp. 67-78.

Lefakane, Dinah. "Old Man River." *Women in South Africa: From the Heart – An Anthology.* Seritsi sa Sechaba, 1988.

Lessing, Doris. *The Four-Gated City.* Knopf, 1969.

Lessing, Doris. *The Grass is Singing.* Michael Joseph, 1950.

Lewin, Hugh. *Bandiet: Seven Years in a South African Prison.* David Philip, 1981.

Lewis, Simon. "Graves With a View: Atavism and the European Vision of Africa." *ARIEL*, vol. 27, vol. 1, 1996, pp. 41-62.

Lindfors, Bernth. "Many Happy Returns? Repatriation and Resistance Literature in a New South Africa." *Current Writing*, vol. 5, no. 2, 1993, pp. 70-79.

Lockett, Cecily, editor. *Breaking the Silence: A Century of South African Women's Poetry.* Ad. Donker, 1990.

Longford, Elizabeth. *Jameson's Raid, the Prelude to the Boer War.* Jonathan Ball, 1982.

Lukacs, G. *Theory of the Novel.* Merlin Press, 1978.

Mackenzie, Craig et al. *Between the Lines: Interviews with Bessie Head, Sheila Roberts, Ellen Kuzwayo, Miriam Tlali.* National English Library Museum, 1989.

Makhoere, Caesarina Kona. *No Child's Play: In Prison under Apartheid.* Women's Press, 1988.

Mandela, Zinzi. *Black as I Am.* Guild of Tutors, 1978.

Mansfield, Katherine. *Collected Stories.* Constable, 1945.

Maracle, Lee. *Sundogs.* Theytus Books, 1992.

Marquard, Jean. "Bessie Head: Exile and Community in Southern Africa." *London Magazine*, vol. 18, no. 9 & 10, 1978-1979, pp.48-61.

Marquard, Jean. "Olive Schreiner's 'Prelude: The Child as Artists." *English Studies in Africa*, vol. 22, no. 1, 1979.

Marchand, Marianne et al., editors. *Feminism, Postmodernism, Development.* Routledge, 2003.

McDonald, Larry. "I Looked for It and There It Was – Gone: History in Postmodern Criticism." *Essays on Canadian Writing*, vol. 56, 1995, pp. 37-50.

McClintock, Anne. "The Angel of Progress: Pitfalls of the Term 'Post-Colonialism'." Williams, Patrick, et al. *Colonial Discourse and Post-Colonial Theory: A Reader*. Columbia University Press, 1994, pp. 291-304.

Meintjes, Johannes. *Olive Schreiner: Portrait of a South African Woman*. Hugh Keartland, 1965.

Miller, J. Hillis. *The Form of Victorian Fiction*. University of Notre Dame, 1970.

Millin, S.G. *God's Step-Children*. 1926.

Mitchell, Juliet. *Psychoanalysis and Feminism*. Penguin, 1974.

Mofokeng, Boitumelo. "Breaking the Silence." *Women Speak: Conference on Women and Writing*. Congress of South African Writers, 1988, pp. 6-10.

Morris, Patricia. "Biographical Accounts of Olive Schreiner." *Olive Schreiner and After*. Edited by van Wyk Smith et al. David Philip, 1983.

Moses, Michael Valdez, ed. "Special Issue: The Writings of J. M. Coetzee." Special issue of *The South Atlantic Quarterly*, vol. 93, no. 1, 1994.

Moss, Rose. *The Schoolmaster*. Ravan, 1981.

Mphahlele, Es'kia. *The African Image*. Faber, 1962.

Mphahlele, Es'kia. "Prometheus in Chains: The Fate of English in South Africa." *The English Academy Review*, vol. 2, 1984, pp. 89-104.

Mukherjee, Arun. "Canadian Nationalism, Canadian Literature, and Racial Minority Literature." *Essays on Canadian Writing*, vol. 56, pp. 78-95.

Mukherjee, Arun. *Oppositional Aesthetics: Readings from a Hyphenated Space*. Tsar, 1994.

Mukherjee, Arun. "Whose Post-Colonialism and Whose Post-Modernism?" *World Literature Written in English*, vol. 30, no. 2, 1990, pp. 1-9.

Munro, Alice. *The Love of a Good Woman*. McClelland & Stewart, 1998.

Murray, Martin J. *The Revolution Deferred: The Painful Birth of Post-Apartheid South Africa*. Verso, 1994.

Murray, Sally-Ann. "Tropes and Trophies: The Lost City Discovered." *ARIEL*, vol. 27, no. 1, 1996, pp. 149-176.

Mutloatse, Mothobi. *Forced Landing*. Ravan, 1980.

Mzamane, Mbulelo Vizikhungo. *The Children of Soweto*. Longman, 1995.

Mzamane, Mbulelo Vizikhungo. "From Resistance to Reconstruction: Culture and the New South Africa." *ARIEL*, vol. 27, no. 1, 1996, pp. 11-20.

Nandan, Satendra. "Beyond the Coups: The Writer and Fiji." *A Shaping of Connections*. Edited by Hena Maes-Jelinek et al. Dangaroo Press, 1989, pp. 69-75.

Ndebele, Njabulo S. "Beyond Protest: New Directions in South African Literature." *Criticism and Ideology*. 2nd African Writers Conference, Stockholm, 1986. Kirsten Holst Peterson, editor. Scandinavian Institute of African Studies, 1988, pp. 205-218.

Ndebele, Njabulo S. "The English Language and Social Change in South Africa." *The English Academy Review*, vol. 4, 1987, pp. 1-15.

Ndebele, Njabulo S. "Redefining Relevance." *Pretexts*, vol. 1, no. 1, 1989. Reprinted in *Rediscovery of the Ordinary: Essays on South African Literature and Culture*. COSAW, 1991, pp. 58-73.

Ndebele, Njabulo S. *Rediscovery of the Ordinary: Essays on South African Literature and Culture*. Congress of South African Writers, 1991.

Ndebele, Njabulo S. "Turkish Tales, and Some Thoughts on South African Fiction." *Staffrider*, vol. 6, no.1, 1984.

Neuman, Shirley, et al. *Labyrinths of Voice: Conversations with Robert Kroetsch*. NeWest, 1982.

Ngcobo, Lauretta. *And They Didn't Die*. George Braziller, 1991.

Ngugi wa Thiong'o. *Decolonising the Mind: The Politics of Language in African Literature*. Currey, 1986.

Ngugi wa Thiongo. *Detained: A Writer's Prison Diary.* Heinemann, 1981.

Ngugi wa Thiongo. *A Grain of Wheat.* Heinemann, 1967.

Ngugi wa Thiongo. *Petals of Blood.* Heinemann, 1977.

Ngugi wa Thiongo. *Weep Not, Child.* Heinemann, 1964.

Nkosi, Lewis. "Fiction by Black South Africans." *Home and Exile.* Longman, 1965, pp. 125-136.

O'Sullivan, W., et al, editors. "*The Collected Letters of Katherine Mansfield* vol. 1. Clarendon Press, 1984.

Okri, Ben. *The Famished Road.* Jonathan Cape, 1991.

Ofeimun, Odia. *The Poet Lied.* Update Communications Limited, 1989.

Olney, James. "Autobiography and the Cultural Moment." *Autobiography.* Edited by James Olney. Princeton University Press, 1980.

Olney, James. *Metaphors of Self: The Meaning of Autobiography.* Princeton University Press, 1972.

Oosthuizen, Ann. *Sometimes When it Rains: Writings by South African Women.* Pandora, 1987.

Parker, Andrew, et al. *Nationalisms and Sexualities.* Routledge, 1992.

Paton, Alan. *Cry, The Beloved Country.* Jonathan Cape, 1948.

Paton, Alan. *Too Late the Phalarope.* Scribner, 1953.

Pearse, Adetokunbo. "Apartheid and Madness: Bessie Head's *A Question of Power.*" *Kunapipi*, vol. 5, no. 2, 1983, pp. 81-93.

Perrakis, Phyllis Sternbrg, editor. *Spiritual Exploration in the Works of Doris Lessing.* Greenwood Press, 1999.

Plaatje, Sol T. *Mhudi.* 1917. Edited by Tim Couzens. Quagga Press, 1975.

Plaatje, Sol T. *Native Life in South Africa.* Ravan, 1982.

Rive, Richard, editor. *Olive Schreiner: Letters 1871-99.* David Philip, 1987.

Robertson, Robert T. "The Hussites: A Pre-History of ACLALS 1945-64." *A Shaping of Connections.* Edited by Hena Maes-Jelinek et al. Dangaroo Press, 1989, pp. 3-7.

Rody, Caroline. "The Mad Colonial Daughter's Revolt: J. M. Coetzee's *In the Heart of the Country.*" Moses, Michael Valdez, ed. "Special Issue: The Writings of J. M. Coetzee." Special issue of *The South Atlantic Quarterly*, vol. 93, no. 1, 1994, pp.157-810.

Ross, Sinclair. *As For Me and My House.* Reynal and Hitchcock, 1941.

Sachs, Albie. "Preparing Ourselves for Freedom." *Spring is Rebellious.* Edited by I. de Kok et al. Buchu, 1990, pp.19-29.

Schreiner, Olive. *From Man to Man.* Fisher Unwin, 1926.

Schreiner, Olive. *The Story of an African Farm.* Chapman & Hall, 1883; Penguin, 1971.

Schreiner, Olive. *Trooper Peter Halket of Mashonaland.* Unwin, 1897; Ad Donker, 1974.

Schreiner, Olive. *Undine.* Benn, 1929.

Schulze-Engler, Frank. "Literature and Civil Society in South Africa." *ARIEL,* vol. 27, no. 1, 1996, pp. 21-40.

Scully, William Charles. *A History of South Africa.* Longmans, 1922.

Sepamla, Sipho. *The Soweto I Love.* Rex Collins, 1977.

Serote, Mongane Wally. *To Every Birth. Its Blood.* Ravan, 1981.

Setuke, Bereng. "Dumani." *Forced Landing.* Ravan, 1980.

Siemerling, Winifred. "Writing Ethnicity: Introduction." *Essays on Canadian Writing*, vol. 57, 1995, pp. 1-32.

Slemon, Stephen. "Reading for Resistance in Post-Colonial Literature." *A Shaping of Connections.* Edited by Hena Maes-Jelinek et al. Dangaroo Press, 1989, pp. 100-115.

Sepamla, Sipho. *A Scattered Survival.* Skotaville, 1989.

Sepamla, Sipho. *Third Generation.* Skotaville, 1986.

Slater, Francis Carey. *The Trek.* Macmillan, 1938.

Smith, Rowland. "The Johannesburg Genre." *Exile and Tradition: Studies in African and Caribbean Literature.* Longman; Dalhousie University Press, 1976, pp. 16-31.

Sole, Kelwyn. "Culture, Politics and the Black Writer." *English in Africa*, vol. 10, no. 1, 1983, pp. 37-84.

Sole, Kelwyn. "Democratising Culture and Literature in a 'New South Africa': Organization and Theory." *Current Writing*, vol. 6, no. 2, 1994, pp. 1-37.

Sole, Kelwyn.. "South Africa Passes the Posts." *Alternation*, vol. 4, no. 1, 1997, pp. 116-151.

Soyinka, Wole. *The Interpreters*. Gardners Books, 1996.

Stead, C.K. *The Letters and Journals of Katherine Mansfield*. Allen Lane, 1977.

Terada, Rei. *Derek Walcott's Poetry: American Mimicry*. Northeastern University Press, 1992.

Ten Kortenaar, Neil. "Beyond Authenticity and Creolization: Reading Achebe Writing Culture."*PMLA,* vol. 110, no. 1, 1995, pp. 30-42.

Thumboo, Edwin. "Commonwealth/New Literatures in a Small Corner of Asia." *A Shaping of Connections*. Edited by Hena Maes-Jelinek et al. Dangaroo Press, 1989, 63-68.

Tiffin, Helen. "Commonwealth Literature: Comparison and Judgment." *The History of Commonwealth Literature*, edited by Dieter Riemenschneider, Narr Verlag, 1983.

Tiffin, Helen. "Post-Colonialism, Post-Modernism and the Rehabilitation of PostColonial History." *Journal of Commonwealth Literature*, vol. 23, no. 1, 1989, pp. 169-181.

Tlali, Miriam. *Footprints in the Quag: Stories and Dialogues from Soweto*. David Philip, 1989.

Tlali, Miriam. "Interview with Cecily Lockett." *Between the Lines*. Craig Mackenize et al., editors. NELM, 1985, pp. 67-85.

Tlali, Miriam. *Mihloti*. Skotaville, 1984.

Tlali, Miriam. *Muriel at Metropolitan*. Ravan Press, 1975.

Tlali, Miriam. *Soweto Stories*. Pandora Press, 1989.

Tshabangu, Mango. "Thoughts in a Train." *Forced Landing*. Ravan, 1980.

Tuchman, Barbara. *A Distant Mirror*. Penguin, 1978.

Tutuola, Amos. *The Palm-Wine Drinkard*. Faber & Faber, 1952.

Van Niekerk, Annemarie, editor. *Raising the Blinds: A Century of South African Stories*. Ad. Donker, 1990.

Visser, Nick. 'Victor Serge and the Poetics of Political Fiction." *Social Dynamics*, vol. 11, no. 2, 1985.

Voss, A. E. "Reading and Writing in the New South Africa." *Current Writing*, vol. 4, no. 1, 1992, pp. 1-9.

Walder, Dennis. *Post-colonial Literatures in English. History, Language, Theory.* Blackwell, 1998.

Walker, Cherryl, editor. *Women and Gender in Southern Africa to 1945.* David Philip, 1990.

Werbner, Richard, et al. *Postcolonial Identities in Africa.* Zed Books, 1996.

Wicomb, Zoë. "Culture Beyond Colour? A South African Dilemma." *Transition*, vol. 60, 1993, pp. 27-32.

Wicomb, Zoë. *You Can't Get Lost in Cape Town.* Pantheon Books, 1987.

Williams, Patrick, et al. *Colonial Discourse and Post-Colonial Theory: A Reader.* Columbia University Press, 1994.

Wood, Philip. "Aporias of the Postcolonial Subject: Correspondence with J.M. Coetzee." Moses, Michael Valdez, ed. "Special Issue: The Writings of J. M. Coetzee." Special issue of *The South Atlantic Quarterly*, vol. 93, no. 1, 1994, pp. 181-95.

Women in South Africa: From the Heart – An Anthology. Seritsi sa Sechaba, 1988.

Wright, B.A. Introduction to John Milton's *Paradise Lost.* Methuen, 1962.

Acknowledgements

The research in this volume was made possible by the following grants:

Social Sciences and Humanities Research Council of Canada-General Research Grant for research on gender, culture and political change in South Africa.

University of Guelph Faculty Development Grant for biographical work on Olive Schreiner.

Human Sciences Research Council of South Africa, Senior Research Grant for biographical research on Olive Schreiner.

The essays and interviews in this volume originally appeared in the following books and journals:

"Interview with Ellen Kuzwayo" first appeared in *Between the Lines.* Cherry Clayton et al., editors. National English Literary Museum, 1989, pp. 57-68.

"Interview with Obi Maduakor" first appeared in *Current Writing*, vol. 11, no. 2, 1999, pp. 136-148.

"Olive Schreiner: Life into Fiction," first appeared in *English in Africa*, vol. 12, no.1, May 1985, pp. 29-39.

"'A World Elsewhere': Bessie Head as Historian" first appeared in *English in Africa*, vol. 15, no. 1, May 1988, pp. 55-69.

"Olive Schreiner and Katherine Mansfield: Transformations of the Outcast Figure by Two Colonial Writers" first appeared in *Short*

Fiction in the New Literatures in English. J. Bardolph, editor. Fuculté des Lettres, 1989, pp. 31-39.

"White Settlers in the Heart of Empire: Visionary Power in Lessing's *The Four-Gated City*" first appeared in *Spiritual Exploration in the Works of Doris Lessing*. Phyllis Sternberg Perrakis, editor. Greenwood Press, 1999.

"Family and State in Prison Narratives by South African Women" first appeared in *New Art and Literature from South Africa*. Kirsten Holst Peterson et al, editors. Heinemann, 1992, pp. 136-144.

"Radical Transformations: Emergent Women's Voices in South Africa" first appeared in *English in Africa*, vol. 17, no. 2, October 1990, pp. 25-36.

"Women's Writing: What's New in South Africa" first appeared in *Southern African Report Archive*, vol. 9, no. 1, July 1993, pp. 1-3.

"White Writing and Postcolonial Politics: Nadine Gordimer and J.M. Coetzee" first appeared in *ARIEL: A Review of International English Literature*, vol. 25, no. 4, October 1994, pp. 153-167.

"Posting South African Letters from Canada" first appeared in *International Journal of Canadian Studies*, vol. 18, Fall 1998, pp. 67-77..

Biographical Note

Ann Clayton was born and educated in South Africa and completed her Ph.D. on Olive Schreiner at the University of Natal in 1985. She taught at the University of Witwatersrand and was Associate Professor of English at Rand Afrikaans University in Johannesburg before moving to Canada in 1990. She then taught English and Women's Studies at the University of Guelph, Ontario.

She has published several volumes of essays and interviews: *Women and Writing in South Africa: A Critical Anthology* (Heinemann, 1989), *Between the Lines: Interviews with Bessie Head, Sheila Roberts, Ellen Kuzwayo, Miriam Tlali* (NELM, 1986), *Speaking of Writing: Conversations with Canadian Novelists* (Vocamus Community Publications, 2017), and *Postcolonial Perspectives: English South African Fiction Under Apartheid* (Vocamus Community Publications, 2017).

She has edited Olive Shreiner's *Thoughts on Woman* (Pretoria State Library, 1985) and *The Woman's Rose* (Ad. Donker, 1986), a collection of Schreiner's stories and allegories. She has also written a new introduction to Olive Schreiner's *The Story of an African Farm* (Ad. Donker, 1986) and edited a casebook of primary and secondary materials about Schreiner, *Olive Schreiner* (McGraw-Hill, 1983).

In addition, she has published poetry and short stories in journals and South African anthologies. Her first collection of poetry, *Leaving Home*, appeared in 1995, and her second, *Migration*, in 2017.

She has been an informal communications volunteer to the provincial government of Ontario and the federal government of Canada since 2002.